JESUS
THE SAME

JESUS
THE SAME

THE COMPELLING CHRIST
YESTERDAY, TODAY
AND FOREVER

CHARLES EDWARD JEFFERSON

Foreword by Sam Laing

DPI
DISCIPLESHIP
PUBLICATIONS
INTERNATIONAL

Edited and Revised from the 1908 edition.
Originally published under the title
The Character of Jesus, New York, 1908,
Thomas Y. Crowell & Company.
Original copyright expired.

This revised edition ©1997
under the title *Jesus—The Same*
Discipleship Publications International
One Merrill St., Woburn, MA 01801

Cover Design: Chris Costello
Interior Design: Chad Crossland

Printed in the United States of America
ISBN 1-57782-041-X

CONTENTS

FOREWORD
Forever Changed

There are many books that have helped me, but only a few have made me who I am. This is one of those. I was introduced to this beautiful, lucid portrait of Jesus some twenty years ago, and I have been forever changed by the majestic, glorious picture of Jesus that it paints. Time after time I have returned to these refreshing, inspiring pages to be renewed in my love for the greatest hero in my life; time after time these words have encouraged me and lifted me up, and have reminded me of the unique, sublime, awesome and thoroughly amazing man who is my Lord. As a result, I have again turned back to live my life as a disciple of Jesus with a heart healed and strengthened and with a passion rekindled and reborn.

I know nothing of Charles Edward Jefferson's life, ministry or theology, except what I have gleaned in passing from this, his portrait of Jesus. He must have been a man who, despite holding to some theological views with which I would probably differ, had a deep love for and understanding of the personality and heart of Jesus. He had a gift for seeing that which most of us overlook and for expressing in lyrical, unforgettable words what he saw.

If you love Jesus and thirst to know Him better, and if you love language and words, you will probably fall in love with this book. I hope this volume becomes for you, as it has for me, a lifetime friend with whom you share some of your most precious hours on earth. Until the Day we see Jesus in heaven with our eyes untainted by unbelief, weakness and sin, we need all the help we can to know, understand, remember, love and adore Him more. I pray that this book will help you toward that noble end.

Sam Laing
Durham, North Carolina

NOTE
from the Publisher

Dr. Charles Edward Jefferson originally preached the sermons collected here in the early 1900s. He published them in 1908. His book, originally released as *The Character of Jesus*, was brought to the attention of Discipleship Publications International by Sam Laing, who has graciously written the foreword for this edition. More than twenty years ago Sam acquired a copy of this book, which, according to our best research, has been out of print for many years. Although we know little about Dr. Jefferson, we found in this work an inspiring and provocative description of Jesus of Nazareth and investigated the possibility of publishing it for a new audience entering the twenty-first century. Having been assured by our attorneys that the original copyright had long since expired, we moved forward with this new edition.

While overall this is a remarkably timeless work, we found it necessary to make some revisions to assist modern readers. In the original work, the author's references to Scripture were usually from the King James Version (KJV) or, on occasion, the author would simply paraphrase. In some cases we have retained his use of the King James Version and have merely added book, chapter and verse after the reference. In other cases when it seemed the KJV wording obscured the meaning, it was replaced with the New International Version (NIV) or the New American Standard Bible (NASB) reference with appropriate notation.

There were very few times words were added to Jefferson's original text, but in such cases, the added words appear in brackets. Sometimes words that are no longer commonly used were changed to words more accepted in contemporary English. In the original version there were no subheadings in the chapters. These we have added, along with an occasional pull quote, to help clarify the material for modern readers.

There are times when we, as editors, had questions about Jefferson's choice of words to describe Jesus. For example, when he calls Jesus the world's greatest optimist (Chapter 9), he uses a word that we would not have chosen. However, it is our feeling that a careful reading of Jefferson's words reveals a balanced and healthy description of Jesus and his faith. While the word "optimist" may not be the best choice, what Jefferson has to say in this chapter does reflect the fact that Jesus saw clearly the darkness of the world, but also had confidence in the ultimate victory of God. A similar observation might be made about other traits of Jesus' character that he describes.

The original work was a good deal longer than what you find here. A few chapters were deleted entirely, usually because the subject matter seemed to be sufficiently covered in other chapters. Portions of other chapters were deleted to make the book more concise.

We wish to give thanks to Barry Maddox of Orlando, Florida, who gave much time to transferring the material from this book to a digital format.

It is our hope and prayer that these words written by one Charles Edward Jefferson nearly a century ago will powerfully remind you of the Jesus who is the same yesterday, today and forever.

Thomas A. Jones
Editor-in-Chief
Discipleship Publications International

PREFACE
to the Original Edition

The following discourses were delivered in the Broadway Tabernacle on Sunday evenings between January first and Easter of the winters of 1907 and 1908, twelve of them in the former year and fourteen of them in the latter. The two opening sermons were preached at the beginning of 1907 and the beginning of 1908, respectively. They are simple studies in the character of Jesus, the threefold purpose of the preacher being to incite professing Christians to a deeper devotion to their master, and to awaken in non-Christians a desire to know more of the founder of the Christian church, and to persuade them to become his followers. The congregations were composed largely of young men, not a few of them being students. It is in response to numerous requests of these young men that the sermons are now published.

INTRODUCTION

"Behold the Man!"
JOHN 19:5 KJV

THE CHARACTER OF JESUS

Let us think together on these Sunday evenings of the Character of Jesus. You will observe the limitation of the subject. Jesus alone is too great a theme to be dealt with in a course of lectures. There are, for instance, the Ideas of Jesus, the principles which he enunciated in his sermons and illustrated in his parables. This is a great field, and fascinating, but into it we cannot at present go. The Doctrines of Jesus, the things he taught of God and the soul, of life and death, of duty and destiny. This also is another field spacious and rewarding, but into it we cannot enter. We might think of the Person of Jesus, meditate upon his relations to the Father and to the Holy Spirit and to us and ponder the immeasurable mystery of his personality—this is what thoughtful minds have ever loved to do. But upon this vast field of thought we also turn our backs in order that we may give ourselves undividedly to the Character of Jesus.

By the "character" of Jesus I mean the sum of the qualities by which Jesus is distinguished from other men. His character is the sum total of his characteristics, his moral traits, the features of his mind and heart and soul. We are to think about his quality, his temper, his disposition, the stamp of his genius, the notes of his spirit and the form of his conduct.

In one sense our studies will be elementary. We are to deal with the ABCs of Christian learning. This is the logical beginning of all earnest study into the meaning of the Christian religion. Before we are rightly prepared to listen to the ideas of Jesus, we must know something of what Jesus is. The significance of what a man says depends largely upon what he is. Two men may say precisely the same thing, but if one is known to be a fool, his words make no impression on us. If the other is known to be wise and good, we give him close and sympathetic attention. A man is better able to appreciate the ideas of Jesus if he first of all becomes acquainted with Jesus' character.

The Scientific Method

To begin with the character of Jesus is to adopt the scientific method of study. The scientist of today insists upon studying phenomena. What he wants is data, and from these he will draw his conclusions. No scientist can begin his work unless put in possession of definite and concrete facts. There is a general opinion abroad that Christianity is something very much in the air. It is vague and nebulous, cloudy and indeterminate, something beautiful as the mist with the morning sun playing on it, but also, like the mist, very thin and high above the world in which men live.

But in this course of lectures I do not ask you to think about visions or conceptions, principles or relations; I call your attention to a few definite and clean-cut facts. This man Jesus was an historic character. He lived his life upon this earth. In his passage from the cradle to the grave, he manifested certain traits and dispositions which it is our purpose to study. If we were to attempt to deal with all his sayings, we should find many of them hard to understand, and if we should attempt to grapple with his personality, we should find ourselves face to face with mysteries too deep to be fathomed. But in dealing with his character we are handling something concrete and comprehensible. Let us place ourselves before him and permit him to make upon us whatsoever impression he will.

'Come and See'

Not only is this the scientific method, it is also the New Testament method. It was just in this manner that the disciples came to know Jesus. They did not begin with the mystery of his person, nor did they begin with sayings which were hard for them to understand. They began simply by coming near him, looking at him with their eyes, listening to him with their ears. It is with a shout of exultation that the beloved apostle in the first of his three letters says, "We handled him with our hands." It would seem from the New Testament that Jesus desires men to come to the truth which he is to give to the world by a knowledge of his character.

When two young men one day followed him along the bank of the Jordan, and he turned upon them and said: "Whom are you looking for?" and they replied, "Where do you live?" his answer was, "Come and see" [John 1:39 KJV]. They remained with him for the rest of the day, and the result of their first meeting was that they wanted their comrades to come and see him also. And from that day to this, the cause of Christianity has advanced in the world simply because those who have already seen him have wanted others to come and share their experience.

Tainted Methods

If this was the method of approach to Christianity in the first century, why is it not the best approach for our time? Christianity in the course of its development has taken on many forms and has gathered up into itself many things which are nonessential. The result is that thousands are bewildered, not knowing what to think or what to do. Many have been offended by Christianity because they have attempted to enter it through the ecclesiastical door. They have come to the religion of Jesus through some professing Christian who has been inconsistent or hypocritical, and simply one such disastrous experience is sufficient sometimes to keep a man away from Christ through his entire life.

Sometimes it is no individual Christian, but the local church as a body that gives the offense. It may be that the church is dead or that its leading men are corrupt or that its preacher is ignorant and does not have the Christian spirit or the Christian outlook, in which case the total impression made by the church is disastrous, and the soul is repelled. There are many men who are not Christians today because it was their peculiar misfortune to come at a critical period in their life in contact with a church which was lacking in Christian sympathy and devotion.

There are others who have attempted to get into Christianity through the dogmatic door. They have come to the dogmatic statements of the Christian church, the doctrines formulated by church councils and theologians, and by these they have been offended. Their reason has been repelled, and their heart has been chilled.

Let me suggest that there is another door: the character of Jesus. Neither professing Christians nor dogmatic statements are the door of the Christian religion. The founder of Christianity says: "I am the Door." It may be that some man in the congregation who has been made cynical by professing Christians, or skeptical by church dogmas may find that he is neither skeptical nor cynical after he has studied the character of Jesus. For after all, to be a Christian is not to be like other professing Christians, or to accept ecclesiastical propositions. To be a Christian is to admire Jesus so sincerely and so fervently that the whole life goes out to him in an aspiration to be like him.

Sign of the Times

This is a very opportune time in which to study the character of Jesus because it is in our day and generation that he has appeared with new glory before the eyes of the world. We who are now living can know him, if we will, better than he has ever been known since the days of the apostles. There have been three stupendous pieces of work accomplished within recent years. Two of them are well known to everybody, the third is recognized by comparatively few.

The first magnificent accomplishment is the construction of the palace of science. This great enterprise has been carried forward by a host of men of genius who have thrown into their work the heroism of prophets and the enthusiasm of apostles. How glorious, how dazzling this palace is, I need not attempt to describe, for it has caught and holds the eyes of the world.

The second great achievement is the development of material civilization. Within these years have come the steamship, the railroad, the telegraph, the telephone and a thousand other inventions by means of which the face of the world has been transformed and the habits of men have been revolutionized. [What would he think of space travel and the Internet?] This is a miracle which is also known to all.

But there is a third piece of work even more wonderful and more far-reaching in its effects than these other two, and that is the work which has been done by a great army of scholars on both sides the sea in bringing Jesus of Nazareth out of the shadows and out of the clouds in which he had been hidden, and placing him once more before the world.

It was in 1835 that Strauss published his first edition of the "Life of Jesus," and from that day to this, the world has been studying the character of the Man of Galilee with an interest which has been constantly deepening, and with a zeal that shows no abatement. The Gospels have been subjected to a scrutiny which has been given to no other writings. The libraries and the mounds and the tombs have been ransacked for manuscripts. The manuscripts have been brought together and carefully

> To be a Christian is to admire Jesus so sincerely and so fervently that the whole life goes out to him in an aspiration to be like him.

compared and each minutest variation has been noted and pondered. Every paragraph has been sifted and every sentence has been weighed; every word has been analyzed and every syllable has been examined and cross questioned. The amount of labor bestowed upon the New Testament is amazing and incalculable.

Men have not been contented with studying the manuscripts. They have studied the land in which Jesus lived; they have measured it from north to south and from east to west with a surveyor's chain. They have taken the heights of the hills and the mountains and the depths of the rivers and seas. With pick and shovel, they have gone down into the earth in search of material to throw additional rays of light upon this man who has made the land "Holy." The first century of our era has been studied as no other century since time began and has been subjected to a scrutiny and analysis which no other civilization has ever known. The customs of the people, their clothing, their houses, every feature of their social and political and ecclesiastical life, everything that they read and everything that they said, and everything that they did has been analyzed, discussed, explained, illustrated, photographed and scattered broadcast in the hope that this might bring men closer to Jesus.

The printing presses on both sides the sea are flooding the world with books about the life and the times of Jesus, and the result is that he looms colossal before the eyes of the world. It is not simply the church that sees him; all men can see him now. He has broken out of ecclesiastical circles; he walks through all cities and lands. All sorts and conditions of men have come to admire him. Those who deny Christian dogmas bow before him. The great unchurched classes who care nothing for anthems or sermons break into applause at the mention of his name. Many of them see him dimly, many have caught only a glimpse of his face and his heart, but everybody knows that he is the man who went about doing good. Everywhere his name is reverenced. It is fitting that in these opening years of the new century we should endeavor to gain a clearer apprehension of the range of his mind and the reach of his heart.

Golden Methods

How are we to get our information? There are six channels through which light will come. We may come to know him through the words he spoke, through the deeds he did, and also through his silences. We may know him also by the impression which he made first upon his friends and secondly upon his foes, and thirdly upon the general body of his contemporaries.

It awes me when I think of the great company that no man can number to which I ask you to join yourselves in this study of the character of Jesus. Let your mind roam over the last nineteen hundred years, and think of the artists who have stood before him, seeing in him new revelations of beauty; think of the poets who have stood before him and have caught inspiration for their songs; think of the musicians who have stood before him and who have worked the impression which he made upon them into tones which lift the heart and set it dreaming; think of the philosophers who have stood before him and meditated on the great ideas which found expression on his lips; think of the unlettered men and women, the great crowd of peasants, plain working people, descendants of the shepherds that heard the angels singing, who have bowed in adoration before him and found rest from their weariness and strength in their weakness. And then let your mind run out into the centuries that are coming and think of the countless generations of men and women who are still to stand before this matchless figure, drinking in inspiration with which to live their life and do their work. If you can see in your imagination this great procession which has been and the greater procession which is yet to be, you will take your places with reverent spirit as once again we attempt to study the character of the man who compels the heart to cry out, "Master!"

REASONS FOR OUR STUDY

Many of you have studied Jesus under the leadership of others, but come with me for a little interval, and let us study him again. The time is ripe for a restudy of his character and career. We have fallen upon distracted and distracting days. The world is crying out for something—it scarce knows what. Wealth has come, but the heart is hungry; knowledge has come, but life for many has slipped into a riddle and delusion. The world is filled with the inventions of human skill and genius, but there is a vast emptiness which neither science nor art is able to fill.

He Makes Life Complete

One of the characteristics of twentieth-century life is discontentment. Some of us are discontented with ourselves. We are restless, unsatisfied, bewildered. We carry with us a consciousness of failure. We feel we are falling short of what we ought to be. Life, in spite of our efforts, is meager and disappointing. Loaded with many possessions we cry, "What lack I yet?"

It may be wise, therefore, to turn aside from the path we have been traveling and listen for a season to Jesus of Nazareth. It may be that he has the secret for which we have been searching. Upon opening the New Testament, the first face which fronts us is his and the first words which greet us come from his lips. He says, "Come unto me and I will give you rest. I am the Bread of Life. I am the Light of the World. If any man thirst, let him come unto me and drink. My peace

I give unto you. You shall receive power. You shall rejoice." Bread and water, light and rest and peace and power and joy. Are these not the seven elemental blessings which make human life complete? If this man promises to give us the things which the soul most desires, it is worthwhile to study his method and find out, if we can, how his proffered gifts can be most speedily obtained. On approaching him we hear him saying: "Follow me! Learn of me! Eat me! Abide in me!" It would seem that he offers us all good things on condition that we become like him. But what is he like? What is his disposition, temper, attitude, nature? Surely all who are discontented with themselves will want to study the character of Jesus.

There are others of us who are discontented, not so much with ourselves as with the world. The time is out of joint, and we are sick at heart because no one seems to be wise or strong enough to set it right. Government is corrupt; the church seems dead or dying; the home is a failure or scandal; society is superficial and tainted; the social order is ready for the burning; the economic system is a burden and curse; the whole framework of the world needs to be reconstructed; and alas, who is sufficient for so Herculean a task? The men with the antidotes are loud-mouthed and confident; the prophets of reform are vociferous and ubiquitous, but unfortunately they do not agree among themselves, and the remedies, when applied, are impotent to cure. The medicines do not seem to be powerful enough, and the doctors stand by the bedside of feverish and delirious humanity, outwitted, discredited, dumfounded. Modern civilization has become a tower of Babel, and the air is so filled with theories of social revision and programs of industrial reorganization that the clearest headed are bewildered by the din and tumult, not knowing in which direction deliverance must be sought.

A Radical Like None Other

When we open our New Testament, we find a man looking at us who, although not a professional revolutionist, has been the cause of many revolutions, and who, although not a disturber of the peace, has repeatedly turned the world upside down. He is not numbered among the radicals because in his radicalism he outstrips them all. He dares to reverse all human standards; confounds the wise by things which are foolish; and confounds things which are mighty by the things which are weak. He has much to say about authority and power, and it is his claim that he can make all things new. The writers of history have confessed that he overturned the Roman Empire and has given to Europe and America a civilization unlike any which the world has ever known.

If his ideas have in them the force of dynamite, and if his personality has power to change the policy of empires, and even the temper of the human heart, it may be that this man is the very man the modern world is looking for in its wild quest for a way of deliverance from its miseries and woes. Surely all of those who are sick of the world as it is and who long for the coming of a world which shall be better, must, if they are wise, come to Jesus of Nazareth for his secret of pulling down the strongholds of iniquity and establishing righteousness and peace on the earth.

> He draws one man to him, infuses into him a new spirit, sends him after one brother man, who in time goes after a third man.

When we study his method, we discover that his supreme concern is for the rightness of heart of the individual man. This molder of empires gives himself to the task of molding individual men. This arch revolutionist starts his conflagrations in the individual soul. He draws one man to him, infuses into him a new spirit, sends him after one brother man, who in time goes after a third man, and this third man after a fourth, and thus does he weld a chain by means of which Caesar shall be dragged from his throne.

Strange as it may seem, he has nothing to say about heredity, and stranger still nothing to say about environment. He keeps his eyes upon the soul, and by changing this he alters the environment and also the currents of the blood down through many generations. When we speak of environment, we think of the physical surroundings: the paving in the street, the sewerage, the architecture of the houses and the lighting of the rooms. We are convinced that with better sewerage and better ventilation and better lighting the plague of humanity would be speedily abated. But this Reformer of Nazareth acts and speaks as though environment is not a matter of brick and plaster, but rather of human minds and hearts. Men are made what they are, not by pavements and houses, but by the men among whom they live.

If you would change the environment, then begin by a transformation of men; and if you would transform men, then begin by a transformation of some particular man. It is by the changing of the character of a man that we change the character of other men; and by changing the character of many men, we change the character of institutions and ultimately of empires and civilizations. When Jesus says, "Behold I make all things new," he lays his hand on the heart of a man. It is out of the heart the demons proceed which tear humanity to pieces, and it is out of the heart that the angels come which restore the beauty and peace of Paradise.

One Heart at a Time

Here then is Jesus' own secret for making an old world over: He will introduce golden ages by giving individuals a character like his own. His character is a form of power mightier than the legions of Caesar or the wisdom of the greatest of the schools. We, who are most discontented with the world and most eager to banish its tyrannies and abuses, may profitably give our days and our nights to the study of the character of Jesus, for through this the burdened world is to pass forward into a brighter day.

There are many fussy and noisy workers, many a blatant and spectacular leader, reformers are often plausible and dashing, and revolutionists impress us by their schemes of creating a world which is new, but after all there is no more effective worker for the world's redemption than the man or woman, who in high or obscure places, strives, in season and out of season, to persuade men to conform their lives to the pattern presented to us in the character of Jesus; and no one is advancing so swiftly toward the golden age as the man or woman who, by prayer and daily effort, endeavors to build up in mind and spirit the virtues and graces of the Man of Galilee.

Here then we find the supreme mission of the Christian minister: It is to help men to fall in love with the character of Jesus. The Bible is an invaluable book chiefly because it contains a portrait of Jesus. The New Testament is immeasurably superior to the Old because in the New Testament we have the face of Jesus. The Holy of Holies of the New Testament is the Gospels because it is here we look directly into the eyes of Jesus. We often speak of the Gospel: What is it? Jesus!

Focus Inward, Not Outward

Let us come now a little closer and ask, What is it in Jesus which is most worth our study? A great deal of attention is being given to the circumstances which formed the framework of his earthly life. Many men are working on the chronology, and others are at work on the geography, and others are interested in the robe and the turban and the sandals. Photographers have photographed every landscape on which he ever looked, and every scene connected with his work or career. Painters have transferred the Palestinian fields and lakes and skies to canvas, and stereopticon lecturers have made the Holy Land the most familiar spot on earth. Writers of many grades have flooded the world with descriptions of customs and houses, of fashions and ceremonies, and amid such a mass of drapery and upholstery, we are in danger of losing the man Jesus.

We may become so interested in the fringes and tassels of his outer life as to miss the secret which his heart has to tell. Many an hour has been spent upon the outer trappings of Jesus' life, which might better have been employed in the earnest study of his mind and heart. Palestine has no interest for us except in so far as it assists us to understand what Jesus was and did. The temporal and local and provincial may be interesting, but it is not important. It is the character of Jesus which has unique and endless significance, and to this then every earnest mind and heart should turn. The pictures have no value unless they carry us deeper into the soul of the man.

It is surprising what meager materials we have to deal with in the study of Jesus. The New Testament writers were not interested in trifles. They cared nothing for his stature, the clothes he wore or the houses he lived in. He had none of the things which biographers are wont to expatiate upon to the extent of many chapters. He had no lineage to boast of. His friends were all obscure. He held no office either in church or state. He had no prestige of wealth and no repute for learning. He was born in a stable, worked in a carpenter's shop, taught for three years and then died on a cross. The external is reduced to its lowest; circumstances are commonplace and meager; the framework of life is narrow and ungilded. The New Testament was written by men who

> The New Testament was written by men who were determined that we should fix our eyes on the man. They wish us to catch the beat of his heart, the swing of his mind, the orbit of his ideas.

were determined that we should fix our eyes on the man. They wish us to catch the beat of his heart, the swing of his mind, the orbit of his ideas. Everything is minimized and subordinated to that which is central and all important: the texture of his spirit and the attitude of his personality. With one accord they cry, "Behold the man!" They want us to know how he looked at things, how he felt toward things, and how things affected him. In a word they want us to know his character. Let us accept their invitation and come and see.

Jesus, Once Again

Some of us have studied this man Jesus for many years. It is we who have the keenest desire to study him again. We shall find in him now things which we have never seen before. The eyes are always changing and the heart expands with the increase of the years. We climb to higher levels of knowledge through study and experience. The time will never come when we shall not relish the study of this man. He is the way to God. It is impossible to become too familiar with the way. He is the express image of the Father's person. The more we study him, the richer is our knowledge of the heart of God. He has declared the Father. The more fully we understand him, the deeper we see into the heart of Deity.

If he and the Father are one, then to know him is indeed life eternal. If he is the author and finisher of faith, we need to see his unclouded face if we are to run with patience the race that is set before us. If we are to be changed from character to character by looking at his character, then every hour is blessed that we spend in making that character clear and beautiful to our heart. The beloved disciple used to say, "We beheld his glory" [John 1:14 KJV]. They gazed upon him as he worked and talked and sang and prayed, and the very memory of what they saw lifted life to new altitudes and dimensions. The ripest and most experienced Christians are readiest to accept the invitation, "Come and see."

Jesus, As for the First Time

Some of us have studied this portrait only a little. Jesus is a name, but, as a person, he is shadowy and unreal. His face has become obscured. Our heart does not feel his power. We are not indifferent to him, but we have no keen sense of loyalty to him, no purifying consciousness of adoration. We need to study him afresh. It may be that as we study him, he will step out of the picture and take his place by our side. Not until we know him as a comrade do we get from him what he has to give. Because his face is dim, we are often depressed and defeated. We are always faint in life's hard places unless we are close enough to catch the light of his eye and feel the strong beating of his unconquerable heart. It may be that to some of us he has been petrified into a dogma. It is a great day for the soul when Jesus stands before it for the first time as a man.

Some of us have scarcely studied him at all. All we know we know by hearsay. We are prejudiced against this Jesus of Nazareth. His face has been distorted partly by the misrepresentations of others and partly by our own idiosyncrasies. It may be that during this study some of us shall see him for the first time as he is.

There are those who do not like metaphysics; let them come and look upon a full-statured man. They do not care for doctrine; let them study a life. They are not interested in dogma; let them fix their gaze upon a person. If the word "revelation" has had to them a mysterious or theological sound, let them contemplate the crowning revelation— the revelation made in the character of a man.

The Gospel Portrait

We shall not discuss the question how the Gospel portrait got here. It is enough for our present purpose to know that it is here. It has been in the world for nearly nineteen hundred years, and through all that period nothing has been added to it and nothing has been taken away. It nourishes faith in God. It keeps the fires of hope and gladness burning on the altar. Men have various theories of the portrait and make different criticisms of it. I ask you to look at it. Other men are looking at it. They are looking at it all round the globe. Millions feel while looking at it that in this portrait they get the largest disclosures of the mind and purpose of the Eternal. It is indisputable that this portrait draws many hearts nearer to God. It may draw you. Only look at it. By looking at it, it may grow also upon you.

Come in Prayer

And may I ask you also to pray while you look. The depth to which you see into a mind or heart depends upon what you bring with you to the contemplation of it. You cannot appreciate the masterpiece of a musician unless you have music in you, or the painting of an artist unless you have in you something of the temperament which the artist has, nor can you understand a character unless you are akin to it in the deepest tendencies and aspirations of your being. The masters of music and art and life reveal themselves only to those who, in some measure, share their spirit.

If you would study the character of Jesus with largest profit, you must respond to that which was dominant in his life. He was preeminently a man of prayer. His was the reverent heart and his look was ever upward. They who pray breathe the atmosphere in which he lived and take the attitude by which they are best fitted to understand his deeds and sayings. In studying a person, spiritual harmony is everything. James lived under the same roof with Jesus but did not understand him. Paul lived far from him but understood him completely. Understanding souls is not a matter of physical proximity or intellectual effort: everything depends on insight and spiritual sympathy. In studying Jesus men ought always to pray and not to faint [Luke 18:1 KJV].

> "These are written, that ye may believe that Jesus is the Christ, the Son of God."
>
> JOHN 20:31 KJV

SOURCES

Where can we find a subject more interesting than the Character of Jesus? It is fascinating to every human being who has the slightest ambition to advance in culture, or who has the smallest capacity for apprehending things which are of deep and enduring significance. Simply as a piece of biography, what a wonderful story this is: How exciting his life; how tragic his death! Whether a man is a Christian or not he must, unless thoroughly hardened by prejudice, take an interest in the life of Jesus.

Lessons from History

No man or woman of intellect can remain unmoved by the death of Socrates. The prison in which he died is one of the holy places of history. So long as men have minds to think and hearts to pity, they will stand in awe before the old Greek philosopher while he drains the fatal cup. But the death of Jesus is more tragic than the death of Socrates.

Who is not interested in the death of Julius Caesar? When will Mark Antony's speech cease to stir the blood? So long as men are human, they will stand awestruck in the presence of that great tragedy enacted in the Roman capitol. But the death of Jesus is more tragic than the death of Caesar.

Moreover, Jesus of Nazareth is the starting point of a thousand influences. The whole world of the last nineteen hundred years becomes unintelligible unless one knows something about him. How can you understand the great art galleries of the world, filled as they

29

are with pictures of his face, and pictures of his mother, and pictures of his disciples, unless you know who he was and what he said and what he accomplished? Step out of the art galleries into the libraries, and how will you understand the great books of history unless you are familiar with his career, for every book is full of his name. Step out of the world of books into the world of men and things; walk along the streets. How will you account for St. Patrick's Cathedral and the Cathedral of St. John the Divine and all the hundreds of churches and missions scattered over this land unless you know something of the man from whose heart they proceeded and by whose name they are known. We have a theme that must be of interest to every human being.

Compact Truth

But as soon as we come to the careful study of the life of Jesus, we are subjected to a series of surprises. The first surprise is that the biography of this man is confined within such narrow limits. If you wish to study the life of Abraham Lincoln, you must consult many volumes. The life of George Washington cannot easily be put into one book. Hundreds of volumes have been written about Napoleon and Frederick the Great and Caesar. But the biography of Jesus is confined to one little book that can be bought for six cents [no longer!] and carried in the pocket. This is the surprising thing: All the story of his life is contained in this one book.

There were many Greek writers living in the days of Jesus, but not one of them wrote his life, so far as any scholar knows. Not a scrap of Jesus' biography at the hands of a Greek poet or historian has come down to us. There were many Roman writers living when Jesus preached in Palestine who were writing on many different personages and on manifold subjects, but not one of them, so far as we know, cared to sketch this man Jesus. There were many professional Jewish writers living in Jesus' day, but so far as we know, not one of them took the trouble to write the story of Jesus' life. This is remarkable! To be sure, there are apocryphal gospels and apocryphal acts and apocryphal epistles and apocalypses, but no one of these, nor do all of them together, throw any light on the character of Jesus which is not furnished by our New Testament. Everything that is positively known of Jesus of Nazareth is confined between the covers of the New Testament.

For years men have been ransacking the libraries, digging up the ruins of ancient cities, and delving into the desert sands, thinking that possibly a page might be found that would throw additional light upon this Man. Years ago two Englishmen, digging in the sands of Middle Egypt, brought up two leaves of papyrus, one of them torn in two. A thrill of delight ran through the world of Christian scholarship at the thought that some new light might be thrown on Jesus' life. Alas! the new papyrus had nothing new to tell. The whole story must be sought within the narrow compass of the New Testament.

But we can bring down the limits to a still narrower area. You can write the life of Jesus from the Book of Acts, but it is a meager life and contains practically nothing not to be found in the Gospels. You may also piece out a life of Jesus from the epistles of the New Testament, but nothing of importance is added to the things already told in the Gospels. And therefore, so far as our present purpose is concerned, we may put aside all the other books of the New Testament and affirm that all which is known of the character of Jesus must be sought for inside the four Gospels. That the life of the greatest and most important man who ever lived upon the earth should be written on pages so small and few is one of the surprises.

Fractions of the Whole

When we study these Gospels, we are surprised that they tell us so little, for they do not give us a complete life of Jesus. They do not tell us how long Jesus lived, but from the scattered hints it would seem that he lived something like thirty-three years. Thirty of these years are passed over with scarcely a word. They are deep sunken in a darkness into which no rays of light enter. The men who wrote the four Gospels did not attempt to deal with ten-elevenths of the life of Jesus. They simply let the larger part alone. Nor did they attempt to deal even with all the three years of his public ministry. They mention what he did or said only on from thirty to thirty-five days. That is, they confine their attention to one thirtieth of his public life, twenty-nine thirtieths being a total blank. Or, in other words, if he lived thirty-three years and the evangelists deal with only thirty-five days, they limit themselves to one three-hundredth part of his earthly career, and allow two hundred and ninety-nine three-hundredths to lie hidden!

These men have recorded many things which he said, but his recorded sayings can be spoken easily within five hours. They tell many things which he did, but nearly all of them might have been crowded into a day, so meager is their report of what Jesus said and did. It is evident, then, that we do not have as much information as we want. The question is, Do we have as much as we need? There is always a wide gap between what we want and what we need, and we need not be surprised that there is a gap here.

These Gospels attempt to give us nothing but his words. They do not give us his facial expression, the quiver of the lip, the glance of the eye. We cannot see his smile or his frown. Facial expression is a revelation, and that revelation is lost forever. Nor do the evangelists attempt to give us his gestures. Gestures are interpreters of thought. A speaker speaks with his head, his shoulders, his hands, and by means of these gestures the thought is unfolded and made clear. Gesture is a revelation, and it is a revelation which has been lost forever. The New Testament does not give us the voice of Jesus. The voice is the best of all interpreters. By its modulations and cadences, by its inflections and

> We are driven to the conclusion that they were writing not the biography of Jesus but the character of Jesus.

emphases, it reveals and explains and illustrates. The music of speech lies in the inflections, and many a word takes on a new glory from the way in which it is spoken. Intonation is a revelation, but in the case of Jesus it is a revelation which has been lost forever.

And then there is another revelation to which we are denied access: the revelation of his sighs and his tears. We cannot see the tears on his cheeks as he looks down on Jerusalem and sobs, "O!" If we could have heard him weeping in the Garden, we could have seen down deeper into his heart. But this revelation is denied us forever. We have nothing but words to deal with, and words are sometimes opaque and ambiguous, stumbling interpreters of the heart. But words are all that God has given us, and with words therefore we must be content.

Words Alone

Right here there springs up a new surprise: We are not to deal with Jesus' words. He spoke in Aramaic, and there are not a dozen Aramaic words left in the Gospels. He said to the little girl, "Talitha cumi" [Mark 5:41 KJV], which being interpreted means, "Damsel, arise!" On the cross he said, "Eli, Eli, lama sabachthani?" which being interpreted means, "My God, my God, why hast thou forsaken me?" [Matthew 27:46 KJV]. Besides these only an occasional Aramaic word has been recorded for us, and with these slight exceptions all the words that dropped from his lips have passed completely away. We read the English New Testament. Its words are not Jesus' words, they are the translators' words, the words chosen by scholars who have interpreted for us the Greek text. But even the Greek words were not spoken by Jesus; the Greek words were translators' words chosen to interpret the meaning of the Aramaic words. It is not unlikely there were Aramaic Gospels before the Greek Gospels were written. But the Aramaic Gospels have long since fallen to dust, and so also have the Greek Gospels. The first Greek copies were written on papyrus, and the papyrus was so frail and fragile that it perished probably in less than a hundred years. We have no copies of the New Testament that run back beyond the fourth century—and this also is a surprise.

Looking, then, at these words with which we have to deal, will they tell us anything of the personal appearance of the Nazarene? Nothing. The men who wrote the Gospels were not interested in the stature of Jesus, in the color of his eyes or hair, in the expression of his face, or the build of his body. The New Testament has been often scrutinized by men eager to get some hint of Jesus' personal appearance, but no such hint has been forthcoming. Expressions here and there have been seized upon and put upon the rack and tortured in order to compel them to give at least a suggestion as to what Jesus looked like. But under torture every sentence of the Gospels remains absolutely silent on this most interesting question.

We must, therefore, at the very beginning banish all pictures of Jesus from our minds. We do not know what he looked like. The artists have not known; they have simply painted from their own imagination. The artists then have simply painted their ideal, and their ideal is the creation of their own heart, and that is what you and I have a right to do. Would you conceive of Jesus as he appeared in the days of his flesh, you must form him according to your own ideal. You have the same right the artists have. This, then, is to be remembered, that we are not to study the personal appearance of Jesus, but the stamp of his mind and the bent of his spirit. In other words, we are to study his character.

Everlasting Impact

But while the smiles and frowns, the intonations and modulations, the glance of the eye and the gesture of the hand, have all been lost and lost forever, we must not think that they were unimportant in the history of the world. All those things helped to make an impression on the men that stood nearest to Jesus. They saw his smile, caught the expression of his eye, heard him laugh, sigh, sob, drank in the music of his voice—and the question is, How were they affected? The New Testament tells us they were affected in two distinct and opposite ways.

Some men were repelled. They disliked him, feared, hated, detested, loathed him. Their loathing became so venomous that they murdered him. They could not allow him to remain upon this earth. That is the effect which he produced upon one type of mind.

There were other men who were attracted by him. They liked him, loved, adored, worshipped him; they were ready to die for him. It should never be forgotten that every one of his disciples, with one exception, laid down his life for Jesus, and that, too, after Jesus was dead. The men who were the nearest to him loved him with an adoration which was boundless, and they communicated the impression to other men, and the impression has come down to this present hour, so that at the beginning of the twentieth century, thousands of miles from Palestine, men are building churches in the name of Jesus, believing that his name is above every name and that every knee should bow to him.

At the very beginning, then, of our study of the character of Jesus, let us remember that Christianity is rooted in a life that was lived upon the earth. There is one part of the Christian creed which every human being can repeat without question and without reservation. There are men who might refuse to repeat the first article, "I believe in God the Father Almighty, Maker of heaven and earth." God is spirit, and a man might refuse to acknowledge that He exists. There are those who might stumble at the last clause in the creed, "I believe in the life everlasting." That also reaches out beyond the sweep of human sight, and there are men who will not affirm beyond that which they can see. But at the very center of the creed there is one little paragraph to which no one can offer reasonable objection, "Suffered under Pontius Pilate, was crucified, died and was buried." There are some who object to the supernatural; they do not like the extraordinary. Very well, let them begin with the ordinary; let them take their stand on the natural. Some of you may think that Christianity is in the air. Its branches, to be sure, are in the air, but its roots are in the earth. Its base is not in philosophy but in human history, not in poetry but in mundane experience. All that you see of Christianity in the world today came out of this man who lived in Palestine, who suffered under Pontius Pilate, was crucified, died and was buried.

May I make of you this one request: While you follow my words, read Mark's Gospel from beginning to end. It is probably the oldest of all the Gospels, the shortest of them all, the most graphic of them all, and seems to come the nearest to Jesus as men saw him in the days of his humiliation. If you will read this Gospel, you will more easily follow me in these studies, and come to know better the one supreme character of history. It is a sad mistake for any man or any woman to leave religious matters entirely to the minister. I cannot study the character of Jesus for you; you must study it for yourselves. All that I can hope to do is to drop suggestions which may possibly assist you in your study.

Better Than Anyone

Possibly somebody may say we cannot write a life of Jesus at all, and that is true, if by "life of Jesus" you mean a complete biography. But what if it should happen that the men who wrote the Gospels were not trying to write a biography of Jesus, but had something entirely different in mind? When Morley wrote the "Life of Gladstone," he filled three ponderous volumes. When Carlyle wrote the "Life of Frederick the Great," he wrote over six thousand pages, filling twenty-one books. When Nicolay and Hay wrote the "Life of Lincoln," they filled ten good-sized volumes.

These Gospel writers evidently did not intend to write a biography of Jesus, otherwise they would not have confined themselves within such narrow limits. We are driven to the conclusion that they were writing not the biography of Jesus but the character of Jesus.

A vast amount of material is necessary for a biography, but only a little material is needed for the elucidation of a character. You do not need all the words a man speaks; just a few of them will answer—every word is a flash of lightning, and like a flash of lightning lights up the world from horizon to horizon. You do not need many deeds; every deed is like a sunbeam touching a dark work into visibility. Despite the fact that the Gospels are so small, we know Jesus, his mind and heart and spirit, better than we know any other man who has ever lived upon the earth. Men who study the New Testament carefully feel that they know Jesus of Nazareth better than any other character of history.

Someone may say, "Ah, Jesus lived two thousand years ago, and therefore we cannot be sure what his character really was." You are mistaken. You can understand a great man better at a distance than when standing near him. No truly great man is ever appreciated at his worth by the people in the midst of whom he lives. The world did not appreciate Abraham Lincoln until he died. His great figure has been looming higher each succeeding decade, and the generations yet to come will understand him better than we do. We understand Luther far better than his contemporaries. We understand the apostles better than the early church fathers did. We understand Jesus of Nazareth better than has any other generation of men that has ever lived.

JESUS
THE SAME

"And they were all amazed."
MARK 1:27 KJV

THE STRENGTH OF JESUS

What was the first impression which Jesus made upon his contemporaries? What has been his first impression on you? Has he impressed you as subdued and meek, calm and effeminate? Have you seen him always as many a painter has painted him: pale and ghastly, sickly, emaciated? When you think of him, do you think of someone thin and gaunt, weak and pallid? Not so did he seem to the people of his day. Open the Gospel according to Mark. In the very first chapter he tells you in four different places what impression Jesus made upon men.

First Impressions

He first tells you of the impression Jesus made on John the Baptist. John was a mighty man, none mightier had ever appeared in Judea; but John said there is coming one mightier than I. When Jesus presents himself to be baptized, a remarkable thing happens. John had called men to repentance; he had faced the greatest men of his day without flinching. He had baptized the great and small, the high and low, the rich and poor, the learned and ignorant. But when this man from Nazareth appears, John falters and draws back and says: "I cannot baptize you. I have need to be baptized by you." Such was the impression which Jesus made upon the intrepid reformer from the desert.

Let us take another illustration: Jesus walks one day along the shore of the Sea of Galilee and sees two men fishing; he says, "Follow me," and straightway they left their nets and followed him. A few steps farther on he sees two other men and says to them, "Follow me," and they left all and followed him. Such was the impression he made upon them.

He goes into the synagogue and begins to teach, and they are amazed, not at what he says, but the manner in which he says it. He teaches them as one having authority and not as the scribes. There is something in his voice that pierces and cuts and thrills, a tone that they have never heard before. It is the note of authority, the note of strength.

Or take another illustration: There is a sick man in the synagogue, and Jesus heals him, and again the people are surprised because God has given such power to a man.

In these four instances the first impression of Jesus is the impression of authority, mastery, power, leadership; he is a man of strength. And that, I think, is the teaching of all the Gospels: They give us repeated illustrations of the power of Jesus. He drew men to him. Wherever he went he was surrounded by a crowd. He goes down to the seashore, and the crowd is so great they push him into the water, so he gets into a boat. He goes to the hilltop, and immediately the hillside is alive with people. He goes to the desert, and immediately a great crowd surrounds him. Sometimes he dares not go into the city because of the tumult which his entrance will certainly stir up. Every city through which he passes is turned upside down by his presence. Only a man of strength draws to him great masses of men.

Schooled and Unschooled

It is noteworthy that widely differing classes of men are drawn to Jesus: the Publicans and sinners, the great unwashed crowd. But Nicodemus, a member of the supreme court of Palestine, also is attracted. And the Roman centurion also is drawn, saying to Jesus, "I know what it is to command and so do you. There is an enemy in my house which I cannot order out; you speak the word and he will depart." Not only did Jesus draw men to him, but he stirred them whenever they came near him. Have you ever noted how many times the evangelists say in speaking of the people: "They were astonished;" "they were astonished with a great astonishment;" "they were amazed;" "they were filled with amazement;" or "they marveled"? The evangelists never say such things of themselves. Matthew never says, "I was surprised." Mark never says, "I was amazed." John never says, "I marveled." They write, all of them, with an arm of marble; there is no feeling in the fingers that hold the pen. They simply write in cold blood the effect which Jesus had on others.

Probably no better illustration of the power of Jesus can be found than that which is afforded in the estimate which different classes of people put upon him. One day when Jesus propounded the question, "Who do men say that I am?" the disciples told him that men had different opinions in regard to him. Some said he was John the Baptist; some said he was Elijah; others said he was Jeremiah; while others, unable to give his exact name, felt convinced he was one of the old prophets. This is remarkable! They went to the grave in order to find a man to whom they could liken him. There was no man then living with whom he could be compared, but we do the same thing. When we want to stir men's hearts, we appeal to the dead; when we search for the great, we descend into the grave and we talk of Shakespeare and Caesar, of Charlemagne and Alfred the Great, of Lincoln and Webster—we dare not use the name of a man living. That is what the Jews did. The name of no man living was great enough to convey their idea of the strength which

> He kindled a devotion that is superior to anything that has ever been known in the world.

they felt resided in Jesus. He was one of the giants of bygone ages who had come back to the earth, carrying with him powers augmented by his sojourn in the realms of death. This tells us clearly that to them he was a man of tremendous power.

And if the Jews felt this in regard to him, what was the impression which he made upon the Roman officials? Pilate is afraid of him. He is the representative of Caesar in Palestine. He is clothed with authority. Jesus is nothing but a poor unarmed peasant. Nevertheless, Pilate is afraid of him. He draws back from him, wrings his hands in uncertainty, washes his hands and tries to get rid of this man. He feels that there is a power in him unlike any power he has ever come in contact with before.

No Middle Ground

But if you would have the finest proof of his power, you can find it in the intensity of the hatred and in the intensity of the love which he excited. How many hated him! They could not hear him talk without sizzling, hissing and boiling like a pot under which the fire roars. He stirred tempests in the heart; he awoke serpents in men. He drove them to madness until they cried out in frenzy, "Crucify him!" Only a great man can do that. You cannot hate a weakling, a ninny. You can hate Nero or Napoleon or any giant, but you cannot hate a nobody. Who was the most detested man in England during the last century? William E. Gladstone. We in America have little conception of the venomous hatred that was poured out upon that man. He stirred men to hatred because he was so mighty. Who are the men most detested in America today? Every one of them is a man of tremendous power. The men that are loathed and feared are men of genius, who have in them extraordinary capacity for bringing things to pass.

But if Jesus drove some men to hate him, he drove other men to love him. He kindled a devotion that is superior to anything that has ever been known in the world. He kindled a fire which ran all over

Palestine, and then around the edges of the Mediterranean, and then into the German forests, which then leaped over the English Channel, and later on it leaped over the Atlantic Ocean, and now it has leaped over all the oceans and is burning more brightly today than ever. And all this conflagration was kindled by his hot heart. These torches which are burning now have been carried down through the blasts of nineteen stormful centuries, and they have never gone out, because he lighted them. He called forth a kind of reverence that has never been granted to any other man who has ever lived. He was so mighty that when men thought of him, they thought of God. The man who stood the nearest to him saw him in a vision after he was gone, and he said, "When I saw him I fell at his feet as dead" [Revelation 1:17 KJV].

"Do not be like the hypocrites."
MATTHEW 6:5 NIV

THE SINCERITY OF JESUS

All the graces are beautiful, but some have a finer loveliness than do others. All virtues are important, but some are more essential than others. Certain virtues are conspicuously ornamental, whereas others are plainly fundamental. Such a fundamental virtue is the virtue of sincerity. It is the keystone in the arch without which the arch collapses. Or to change the figure, truthfulness, honesty, plainness, frankness, simplicity, these and many others are only children of the Queen: sincerity.

It is the virtue which the human heart instinctively craves and looks for. It is a trait which a parent's eyes seek for in his children. Anything like deceit or trickery or sham in a child causes the parental heart to bleed. "Do you mean what you are saying?" "Are you telling me what you really feel?" "Are you concealing from me things which I ought to know?" There is nothing which a parent desires so much in his children as the unaffected simplicity of a sincere heart. This is what we demand in all the higher relationships of life. A man may sweep the pavement or make our garden and do both well, though he is at heart a cheat. But we like him better and we feel more comfortable in his presence if he looks at us out of honest eyes.

True Friendship in a Fallen World

There is an adjective with which the word "friend" will not keep company and that is the adjective "insincere." Sincerity is the very blood and breath of friendship. "Pure gold he is," we say with exultation, meaning that in our friend there is no alloy. His nature is unspoiled and unadulterated. The very suspicion that someone whose life is close to us is insincere renders us restless and makes the universe seem insecure.

And yet how common insincerity is. What a miserable old humbug of a world we are living in, full of trickery and dishonesty and deceit of every kind. Society is cursed with affectation; business is honeycombed with dishonesty; the political world abounds in duplicity and chicanery, and there is sham and pretense and humbuggery everywhere.

Yes, it is a sad, deceitful, demoralized world in the midst of which we find ourselves; but thank God there are hearts here and there upon which we can evermore depend. We have tested them, and we know them to be true. Life would not be worth the living if there were no one on earth sincere. It is to the honest heart that we return again and again, seeking rest and finding it. There are some things we cannot be, and many things which we cannot do. But this one thing is within the reach of us all—we may pray to God unceasingly to keep our heart sincere.

If you would see sincerity in its loveliest form, then come to Jesus. Here is a man incapable of a lie. Nothing was so abhorrent to him as falsehood. No other people so stirred his wrath as men who pretended to be what they were not. The most odious word upon his lips was the word "hypocrite." Have you ever wondered why it is impossible to speak that word without it falling from the lips like a serpent? It is because his curse is resting on it. It was not a harsh word before he spoke it, but he breathed the hot breath of his scorn into it, and it has been ever since a word degraded and lost.

A hypocrite is an actor. It is a word taken originally from the stage. In the theater we expect men and women to be other than they seem to be. An ordinary plebeian wraps round him the robes of a king, talks like a king, and acts like one, and we are not offended, because we are not deceived. It is expected that on the stage no one shall seem to be what he really is. But on the great stage of the world, God expects every man to be what

> The political world abounds in duplicity and chicanery, and there is sham and pretense and humbuggery everywhere.

he claims to be. If we say things we do not believe, and profess things we do not feel, and lay claim to things which we do not possess, we are tricksters and deceivers, causing mischief and confusion in the world. It was the sincerity of Jesus which drove him into deadly conflict with the hypocrites. A hypocrite and Jesus cannot live together.

Nothing but the Truth

It was his constant exhortation that men should speak the truth. The religious leaders of his day had divided oaths into two classes: one class binding, the other not. If an oath contained the name of God, it was binding on the conscience; if for God's name some other name was substituted, then the conscience might go free. Jesus was disgusted by the reasoning of the bat-eyed pettifoggers. "Do not swear at all" [Matthew 5:34 NIV], he said. "Let your 'Yes' be 'Yes,' and your 'No,' 'No'" [Matthew 5:37 NIV]. In other words, "If you want to render a thing emphatic, simply say it over again. If men doubt you, then quietly repeat what you have already declared." It was the belief of Jesus that a man's word ought to be as good as his oath, or as we say, "as good as his bond." If the world were the kind of world God wants it to be, then all the evidence that would be needed to prove a certain thing true would be that a man had asserted it. If it is necessary now in courts of justice to make use of oaths, that is because of the Evil One who has corrupted many hearts and rendered the ordinary speech of humanity unreliable. In an ideal world all oaths are unnecessary and unthought of.

It was because of Jesus' incorruptible sincerity that we have from his lips such a remarkable outpouring of plain words. You and I do not like plain words. We dare not use them—at least often. We water our words down. We pull the string out of them. We substitute long Latin words for plain, short, Anglo-Saxon words, for by multiplying the syllables we attenuate the meaning. For instance we say "prevarication" instead of "lie," because falsehood, when expressed pompously, loses its evil and grossness. But Jesus would not use words of velvet when words of velvet flattered and deceived. It was his work to help men see themselves as they were. He characterized them by words which accurately described their character. One day he told a crowd in the city of Jerusalem that they were of their father the devil, and that the lusts of their father they were eager to do. He went on to add that the devil was a murderer and that he abode not in the truth because the truth was not in him. We are shocked by such plainness of speech. We do not like it. Is that because we dare not express things as they are? Have we gotten into the habit of hiding our eyes and trying to make black things seem gray or even white?

> **Jesus' unquestioned loyalty to truth gives his words a value which no other words possess.**

Jesus was incorrigibly sincere, and it was sincerity which drove him to tell men the plain truth. He said to these men, "If I should say I do not know God, I should be a liar like you." There was a strong inducement for him to conceal his extraordinary knowledge. A man makes himself odious by claiming to know more than other men, and by asserting that he can do more than anybody else. It would have been easier for Jesus to adopt the language of the professionally

humble people who are always saying that they do not know anything and cannot do anything and do not amount to anything. But
Jesus was a man of truth. He could not disguise the fact that his knowledge was unique and that his power was unparalleled. Because he
was true, he could not hold back the fact that he was the Good Shepherd and the Door, the Bread of Life and the Light of the World. Nothing but sincerity would ever have driven him to outrage the feelings
of his countrymen by assertions so extraordinary. Had he kept silence
or pretended to be ignorant on matters on which he possessed full
knowledge, he would indeed have been a liar like the very men with
whom he was struggling. All these remarkable declarations of his in
regard to the nature of his personality and the range of his power
were forced from his lips by a heart unswervingly loyal to the truth.

The Frightful Truth

The warnings of Jesus have often aroused criticism and condemnation because of their severity and the frightening words in which
they are expressed. He told certain men they were moving onward to
perdition and painted their loss and ruin in phrases which have caused
the human heart to shudder. How will you account for such vigor of
language? It was certainly cruel to speak such words if he did not
know the possibilities and doom of sin. If he knew, then he was bound
to tell. The awful parables of the New Testament are the product of a
heart that was uncompromisingly sincere. To speak soft words to
men whose feet are hastening down the road to ruin, how was it
possible to do it?

His very sincerity drove him into language which, to our cold
hearts, seems exaggerated and needlessly abusive. He called the
leaders in Jerusalem liars, blind men, fools, serpents, vipers. If they
were not all this, then Jesus stands condemned for making use of
such cutting words. But suppose these men were precisely what
such words described. Then what? Suppose they were, in very fact,

liars and fools and blind men. Was it not the duty of Jesus to inform them of their pitiable condition? What else could a sincere friend do? These men supposed they could see and were wise, but if they were mistaken, was it not incumbent on an honest man to deliver them, if possible, from their delusion? If they were venomous and deadly and treacherous, why should they not be likened to serpents and vipers? There is not a trace of bitterness in Jesus' language. It is the calm statement of a horrible fact. The Lord of truth must, of necessity, use words which accurately characterize the persons who are to be instructed and warned.

The inmost heart of Jesus finds utterance in his declaration to Pontius Pilate that he had come into the world to bear witness to the truth. That was his work. He never shirked it. He never grew weary in doing it. He was surrounded all his life by men who bore witness to falsehood. They lied about him in every city in which he worked. They misrepresented his deeds and his words and motives. They filled all the air with lies. The witnesses who appeared against him at his trial were liars. But in the midst of the despicable set of false-minded, false-hearted maligners and murderers he stood forth, calm and radiant, as the one man in all the world whose lips had never been sullied by a falsehood and whose heart had never been stained by a lie.

The Drawing Power of Truth

In the centuries which have passed since Jesus died, many strange and uncomplimentary things have been said about him, but it is surprising how loath men have been to accuse him of deceit. They have been willing to say he was mistaken. They have called him a visionary, a fanatic, an enthusiast, and dreamer; but no man of sane mind or heart has ever ventured to assert that Jesus of Nazareth was an intentional deceiver. Men have claimed that his apostles were rogues and falsifiers, that they deliberately misrepresented both his person and his teaching; but no one has dared to argue that Jesus himself was capable of a lie. There is something so pure and frank and noble about him that to doubt his sincerity would be like doubting the brightness of the sun.

Jesus' unquestioned loyalty to truth gives his words a value which no other words possess. When we listen to the words of other men, we must make subtractions and allowances. No man puts his whole self into his speech. His words reveal him and they also conceal him. There is a discrepancy between the soul and what the mouth declares. Not so with Jesus. He holds back nothing. What he thinks he says; what he feels he declares. He declares all things as they are. He is not swerved by sin within nor cowed by hostile forces from without. His character is revealed in his speech. A Chinese proverb says that words are the sounds of the heart. This is certainly true of the words of Jesus. His words are simply the pulsations of his heart. They are unlike any other words ever spoken. They contain the full-statured spirit of a man. In these words this great soul comes out and stands before us, and in them we behold his glory.

This, then, is the man we want. A man like this can be a refuge in the time of storm. To him we can flee when sick at heart. Because of the deceptions of the world, we cry out in wretchedness, "Who shall show us any good?" When men disappoint us and friends are few, we can come to one who says, "I am the truth." When we are weary and heavy laden, we can rest our souls upon one who is as certain as the morning and as faithful as the stars. The world is filled with jangling voices, and it is hard to know which voice to trust; but his voice has in it something which inspires assurance and quenches uncertainty and doubt. What he teaches about God we can receive. What he says of the soul we can believe. What he declares of sin and the penalty of sin we can accept. What he tells us of the soul we can depend upon. What he asserts concerning the principles of a victorious life we can act upon, never doubting. When he tells us to do a thing, we can do it, assured that that is the best thing to do. When he warns us against a course of action we can shun it, knowing that in that direction lie night and death. The path which he exhorts us all to take we can take with boldness, convinced that if we take it we shall arrive safe at home at last.

"And from then on no one dared
ask him any more questions."

MARK 12:34 NIV

THE POISE
OF JESUS

By the poise of Jesus I mean the fine balance of his faculties, the equilibrium of his nature. Every boy knows what it is to balance a cane on his hand, or to poise a cane by resting one end of it on the tip of his finger. After a little practice it is possible for him to hold the cane absolutely straight. This equilibrium is a state of rest brought about by the counteraction of two or more opposing forces. Just so a man can poise himself in the midst of the storms of this boisterous world. This equilibrium is due first of all to a certain balance of faculty. How rarely do we find well-balanced men! The average man is one-sided, unsymmetrical, unevenly developed. We are all overdeveloped on one side of our nature and underdeveloped on the other. It seems to be well-nigh impossible to keep our faculties in even balance. If we are strong in certain characteristics, we are practically certain to be weak in the opposite characteristics. Look around upon the men and women that you know, and in how may of them can you say that their disposition is finely balanced? "Oh, if he did not have so much of that!" "Oh, if he only had a little more of this!" That is what we always feel when the characters of men pass before us for judgment. "He would be an ideal man, but...." "She would be a queen among women, but...." There is always just a little something lacking to make the character what it ought to be.

Avoiding All Extremes

But when we come to Jesus, we find ourselves in the presence of a man without a flaw. He was enthusiastic, blazing with enthusiasm, but he never became fanatical. He was emotional—men could feel the throbbing of his heart—but he never became hysterical. He was imaginative, full of poetry and music, seeing pictures everywhere, throwing upon everything he touched a light that never was on land or sea, the inspiration and the poet's dream, but he was never flighty. He was practical, hard-headed, matter of fact, but he was never pro-saic, never dull. His life always had in it the glamour of romance. He was courageous but never reckless, prudent but never a coward, unique but not eccentric, sympathetic but never sentimental. Great streams of sympathy flowed from his tender heart toward those who needed sympathy, but at the same time streams of lava flowed from the same heart to scorch and overwhelm the workers of iniquity. He was pious, but there is not a trace about him of sanctimoniousness. All the oily disgusting piety which has been caricatured in the books is the product of undeveloped hearts and minds far removed from the piety of his robust soul. He was religious, the most profoundly religious man that ever turned his face toward God, but never once did he slip into superstition. And because he is so well rounded and on every side so complete, men have never known where to class him. Of what temperament was he? It is impossible to say. He had in him all the virtues, and not one of them was overgrown. He exhibited all the graces, and every one of them was in perfect bloom. He stands in history as the one man beautiful, symmetrical, absolutely perfect.

Out of this balance of his powers comes his unrivaled poise in conduct. He lived always in a whirlwind. While men bent like reeds around him, he never so much as wavered. Men laid their traps and tried to catch him, but he walked bravely in the midst of them and never was entrapped. The intellectual athletes of his time tried to trip him, but they never did. His enemies did their best to upset him, but they never could. They flung their lassos at his head, but they never got a lasso around his neck. They dug their pits, but he never tumbled into them. Wherever he went he was surrounded by enemies waiting to catch him in his talk, but they never caught him. They asked him all sorts of questions, expecting that by his answers he would incriminate himself, but he never did. They brought out to him one dilemma after another, saying "We will catch him on one horn or the other," but he escaped them every time. After they had done their best, they retired, vanquished from the field. He remained undisputed conqueror.

This wonderful poise came out in the temple when he was only a boy of twelve. The old men in the midst of whom he sat were astounded at his answers. At the beginning of his public career he heard the seductive voices sounding in his ears. Time and again the evil one came to him with a new allurement, but every time he hurled the tempter back by quoting just the passage of Scripture which that temptation needed. Men tried to convict him of breaking the law in regard to the Sabbath day, but instantly he proved from Scripture and from reason that what he did was right. Men interrupted him in the midst of his

> He had in him all the virtues, and not one of them was overgrown.

preaching, but he was never disconcerted. "Make my brother," cried a man, "divide the inheritance with me." And quick as a flash the answer came: "Who made me a ruler over you? Let me tell you, and everybody else, to beware of covetousness." When Peter at Philippi began to protest against his going to Jerusalem where he would be killed, Jesus said, "Get thee behind me, Satan" [Matthew 16:23 KJV]. He had heard that voice before. He recognized it even on the lips of his friend. It is one of the devil's last resources to speak through the mouth of a friend, but such a trick cannot deceive Jesus.

Silencing His Accusers

On the last Tuesday of his life, they determined to undo him. All the different parties united their forces and put their heads together and concocted schemes by means of which this young prophet should be brought to prison. The Pharisees go to him with this question: "Is it lawful to pay tribute to Caesar?" It was an insidious question. If he said yes, then that would make him hateful to every patriotic Jew, for no Jew who had a patriotic heart believed it was right to pay Jewish money into a Gentile treasury. If, on the other hand, he said no, then he proved himself to be a traitor to Rome, and the Roman officials could immediately pounce down on him. What will he do? Holding a piece of money in his hands he says, "Whose superscription is this?" And when they say "Caesar's," he hands the money back to them, saying, "Render to Caesar the things that are Caesar's and to God the things that are God's" [Mark 12:17 KJV]. The Pharisees were conceited people, but after that they dared not ask him more questions.

However, there was a scribe who thought he would try his hand. "What is the great commandment of the law?" he said, to which Jesus replied, "Love the Lord thy God with all thy heart and thy neighbor as thyself." "But who is my neighbor?" And then Jesus told him about the priest and the Levite and the Samaritan who saw the man by the wayside. After he had told the story he thrust his question into the man's heart: "Which one of the three was neighbor to the man who fell among the robbers?" After that the Scribes asked him no more questions.

The time comes when Jesus is seized and carried before Caiaphas, and the marvelous poise of the prophet disconcerts and dumfounds the high priest. Unable to do anything with him, he sends him to Pilate. Pilate questions him and becomes afraid of him. What a picture! The prophet of Galilee calm, immovable, saying, "To this purpose was I born, and for this came I into the world, to bear witness to the truth." See Pilate cringing, cowering, shuffling, washing his hands and saying he does not propose to have anything to do with such a man. Jesus has poise, and Pilate, representative of the Eternal City, servant of an empire of blood and iron, has no poise at all. It is an interesting fact that even though Jesus was speaking constantly in public for three years, not one of his enemies was able to catch him in his speech, and when at last they convicted him, they had to do it on a trumped-up lie.

It also is noteworthy that not one of the enemies of Jesus was able, by unfairness or falsehood or hatred, to push Jesus into a hasty word or an unrighteous mood. Most men are so poorly balanced that you can push them with very little pressure into sinful speech or an un-Christian disposition. Jesus was so firmly poised that under the pressure of the most venomous vituperation that has ever been hurled against a man, he stood unmoved and unmovable. His poise was divine.

Timeless Attraction

Because he is so well balanced and so finely poised, each succeeding generation comes back to him for inspiration. Is it not remarkable that the men of the first century thought they saw in him the ideal figure of what a man should be; and that men in the fourth century looking at him felt the same; and that men in the tenth century looking at him felt the same; and that men in the sixteenth century looking at him agreed with all the centuries that went before; and that men in the twentieth century looking at him feel that in him they find a perfect pattern?

Men of intellect who live the intellectual life look to him for guidance and instruction. Men of emotion who desire to replenish the springs of feeling look to him for inspiration. Men of high aspirations who desire to lift the soul sit humbly at his feet, confessing that he has the words of life. And now that new and complicated problems have arisen in commercial life and industrial life and social life, men are turning wistfully toward him, feeling that he has the key which will unlock all the doors, that he knows the secret of a complete and per-fect life. There is a grace about him which does not fade; there is a sanity about him which compels respect; there is a charm about him which woos and wins the heart; and we, like preceding generations, fall down before him acknowledging that his character is without a flaw and that his life is without a blemish.

4

"I make all things new."
REVELATION 21:5 KJV

THE ORIGINALITY OF JESUS

The word "originality" does not occur in the New Testament, for no one in Jesus' day ever raised the question of whether he was original or not. Everyone took it for granted that he was. Wherever he went, the eyes of men opened wide. Palestine had become a drowsy place, but Jesus, by his teaching, shook it out of its lethargy and sleep. Wherever he went, men were stirred to fever heat by what they saw and by what they heard and cried out in astonishment, "We have never seen it after this fashion."

His teaching itself struck Jesus' contemporaries as novel. "A new teaching!" was the exclamation which followed many of his discourses. It was the opinion of his severest critics that no man had even spoken as he was speaking. There was something in the manner, as well as in the matter, which arrested attention and threw a fresh light upon God and men.

There had been many a teacher in Palestine, but not one of his predecessors had spoken with his accent. The common people observed at once that his manner was not the manner of the professional teacher of the land. He taught them as one who possessed authority.

Truly Different

The man himself, men soon saw, was different from other men then living. Sometimes they imagined he might indeed be one of the giants of the early centuries returned to the earth again, and at other times they could offer no explanation for his genius, simply exclaiming, "What manner of man is this!" [Mark 4:41 KJV]. It was because Jesus was different from all other men of his day and generation that he created a sensation which left the nation quivering. If he had repeated the old teachings in the old fashion, he would not have infuriated the Scribes and Pharisees and brought about the tragedy of Golgotha. He was too original to be endurable. He advanced too many strange and revolutionary ideas to make it safe for the land to hold him. It was because he made all things new that they nailed him to the cross.

Was Jesus really original? This subject of originality is always provocative of discussion. No man has ever claimed to be original whose claim has not been disputed. No genius has ever been placed among the thinkers of the world without stirring up a host of critics who have vehemently denied his right to a place there.

Was Jesus then original? It depends on what you mean by originality. If to be original one must coin words never heard before and speak in phrases which no other tongue has ever used, then Jesus was not original. He coined no new words, and many of his phrases have the flavor of earlier times. Nor was he the proclaimer of ideas that had never entered man's mind before. All his main ideas of God and the soul, of duty and of destiny had been, if not expanded in the writings of the Hebrew poets and prophets, at least suggested there; and the principles of conduct which Jesus taught were, for the most part, the very principles which had been proclaimed by men of God before his day.

If there is a God who loves our race, it is incredible that no correct idea of Deity or the soul, of duty or of destiny, should have entered the human mind before Jesus was born in Bethlehem. Sad indeed it would have been had Jesus, on coming to the earth, found no conceptions in men's minds which corresponded to the truth and no feelings in their hearts which God could take delight in. The fact is that God has never left himself without a witness. The Son of God has always been in the world. He is the light that lights every man who is born. From the beginning he has been giving men right ideas and right feelings and helping them to reach right conclusions and decisions. We ought, there-fore, to expect nothing in Jesus' teaching absolutely unthought of before his incarnation. We ought to expect to find just what we do find, that everything he taught had been anticipated and that all his cardinal ideas had existed in germ in the writings of holy men who at various times had been moved by the Holy Spirit.

> No personality like that of Jesus had ever been encased in flesh before. He was a new man. Even Roman soldiers could feel that he was different from every other man they had ever known.

Not to Destroy but to Fulfill

Jesus, instead of suggesting ideas never before heard of and ex-pounding truths of which no man had ever conceived, picked up the ancient writings, declaring that they contain the word of the Almighty and that he had come to interpret their meaning and to fulfill what the poets and prophets had dreamed. He did not come to destroy the old ideas or the old truths. He came to fill full. There had been foreshadowings and anticipations and approximations, and now, in the fullness of time, God is going to speak His full-toned message through His Son.

It is at this point, then, that we are to look for the originality of Jesus. We shall not find it in his phrases, or even in his conceptions, but rather in his emphasis and his manner of reading life and the world. He began by reading an old chapter in Isaiah, but he gave it an emphasis which it had never known before, the result being that it burst upon the congregation in Nazareth with the force of a fresh revelation. Men were reading the Scriptures, but they did not know which words to emphasize. Jesus understood. The result was that the Scripture became new.

Religion is partly ceremony and partly ethics. Like all things else on earth, it must have a body and also a spirit. But the leaders of the Jewish church had forgotten the point of emphasis. Jesus knew. By emphasizing mercy instead of sacrifice, he made religion new. Men had forgotten how to read the world. There were institutions and there were human beings, and the wisest men of Israel had forgotten which is most important—an institution or a man. Jesus threw the emphasis on the individual soul and by so doing opened a new epoch in the history of the world.

Absolute Confidence

There was also an accent in his teaching which men had never heard before, not even in the voice of Moses or Elijah. It was the accent of assurance, certainty, authority. It is not the words which a man speaks, but the way in which he speaks them which determines their effect upon the life of the world. No such an accent as that of Jesus had ever before been heard in Palestine. There was never a quiver in his voice. In no discourse was there anything problematic. He never hesitated, speculated or made use of intonations which indicate a wavering mind. He was always positive, certain, infallible. "Verily, verily, I say unto you." ["I tell you the truth."] Such was the manner of his speech, and it was a manner which he caught from none other.

The new accent and the new emphasis were the product of a new personality. No personality like that of Jesus had ever been encased in flesh before. He was a new man. Even Roman soldiers could feel that he was different from every other man they had ever known. He had all the faculties and passions of our common humanity, and yet no one had ever had them in the combination and in the strength in which they were found in him. Jesus was man completed. What a fullness of life was in him! What a power he had! The world of nature responded to the gentlest touch of his fingertips. He was different from all other men that had ever been, and he said so.

Unique Claims

He lifted himself into a unique position and claimed for himself privileges and rights which he denied to all others. He claimed to be the Light of the World, the Bread of Life, the Water of Life, the only Good Shepherd, the Way, the Truth, the Life, the only mediator between God and man, the only one who knows deity completely and who can save the world from its sins.

Here we strike something which is unique and in every sense original. No other man had ever spoken after this fashion either in Palestine or out of it. No language like this was ever heard in India or anywhere else. There is nothing even resembling this in the greatest of the Hebrew poets or prophets. It is when Jesus speaks of himself that we catch an original note in the music of our world. When you hear someone challenging the originality of Jesus and talking about the parallel passages to be found in the rabbinical writers, ask for a few parallel passages corresponding to the paragraphs in the Gospels in which Jesus declares what he is.

John, who knew him best, heard him saying, "I make all things new" [Revelation 21:5 KJV]. He could say this because he was new himself. Not having our infirmities and fears, our frailties and our sins, his eyes see things as ours do not see them, and his heart has feelings which we but dimly understand. He says, "Come to me, and I will make all things new!" He does it by giving us a changed attitude to life, by teaching us how to shift the emphasis from words unimportant to words important, and by showing us the insignificance of show and form compared with the qualities of a loving heart. It is an original work, and only he can do it. He did it for Paul. Paul was a scholar and was familiar with those wonderful rabbinical writings in which certain modern scholars find such stores of treasures. But for some reason these wonderful writings, even when taught by the greatest of rabbis, did not reach the core of Paul's need, and he kept on crying, "What a wretched man I am! Who will rescue me from this body of death?" [Romans 7:24 NIV]. And then one day he met Jesus, and behold, all things became new. From that day to the day of his death, Paul urged men to put off the old man and to put on the new man, which, after God, is created in righteousness and true holiness.

Life-Changing Perspective

It may be that for some of you life has grown irksome and the world drab and commonplace. Life has lost its sparkle and its zest. The days are threadbare and everything has lost its bloom. What will you do? This is the wise thing to do: Go to Jesus and give yourself afresh to him. Sink your life deeper into his life and catch his ways of seeing things and serving God. Take his standpoint; assume his attitude; catch his emphasis; drink in the accent of his voice; and undoubtedly, he will do for you what he did for Saul of Tarsus and what he has done and is doing still for many—he will make all things new. He unifies human life and simplifies it and elevates it and transforms it and transfigures it, all because he is the Master and the Savior of the heart. "If any man be in Christ, he is a new creature: old things are passed away; behold, all things are become new" [2 Corinthians 5:17 KJV].

5

"Narrow is the way."

MATTHEW 7:14 KJV

THE NARROWNESS OF JESUS

Let us think about the narrowness of Jesus. I know it is a disparaging word in our modern speech and damaging to a person's reputation. We often hear it used in a sinister and condemning sense; we sometimes use it so ourselves. We say, "Oh, yes, he is narrow," meaning that one side of his nature has been blighted, blasted. His mind is not full orbed. His heart is not full grown. He is a dwarfed and stunted man, cramped by a defective education or squeezed out of shape by a narrowing environment. In no such sense as this was the man of Galilee narrow. But what word will better express one of the conspicuous traits of Jesus than just this word "narrowness"? He set definite boundaries for himself; he shut himself up within contracted limits—in this sense he was narrow.

How narrow was the circle inside of which he did all his work! He lived his life in Palestine, a little country no larger than Connecticut. It was not a prominent country either, but only a little province tributary to mighty Rome. It cut no figure in the eye of the world, and the lords and ladies of the world's capitals knew little of it and cared less. It was an obscure and rural country, small in territory and insignificant in prestige, and yet the Prince of Glory confined himself to this little corner of the earth.

He might have traveled across the world as many an illustrious teacher had done before his day. He might have taught in Athens and lifted up his voice in the streets of Rome—the Eternal City. He might have given his message to a wide circle of men whose influence covered many lands; but he rather chose to stay at home, to give his time to the cities of Galilee, to pour out his strength on the villages of Judea. For thirty years he remained in the dingy obscurity of a carpenter's shop, and the country upon which he poured out the full wealth of his brain and heart was only a carpenter's shop among the palaces of the earth.

One Thing

If his field was contracted, so also was the character of his work. He only tried to do one thing. There were a thousand good things which a good man in Palestine might have done, but he left nine hundred and ninety-nine of them unattempted and confined himself to the one thing which he believed his Heavenly Father had given him to do. Men did not understand such narrowness. They were always urging him to swing into a wider orbit and do something which would create a greater stir. A man one day interrupted him while he was speaking, saying, "Make my brother divide the inheritance with me!" But his reply was, "That lies outside my province—come and listen to me and I will do for you the service which God has appointed me to do." It was a righteous piece of work which the man wanted to have done, but it was not Christ's work, and therefore he would not do it. No one man can do everything. There are a thousand things which need to be done and yet which no man, however industrious and noble, can perform. Jesus set limits to his activity, and beyond those limits no man ever persuaded him to go.

One day his brothers wanted him to go to Jerusalem and make an impression on the big men there, but he refused to listen to their exhortation, telling them that they might go any time they chose, but that it was different with him. He could not go until it was time for him to go, until his work compelled him to go. He could not go until his hour had come. When the hour arrived, he set his face steadfastly to go to Jerusalem. All along the way men tried to divert him, but he could not be diverted. To Jerusalem he must go. He had a baptism to be baptized with, and he was pressed in on both sides, and there was no relief until his work had been accomplished. He always speaks like a man whose

> He had eyes which saw through the exterior of men's hearts, and he judged them with a fearlessness which made them crouch in terror.

feet are on a narrow path. He could not dissipate his energy; he could not waste a single hour. It was always, "I must," "I must," "I must." There were broad roads on his right and left, and along these roads thousands of his countrymen were traveling, but he could not go with them. It was for him to walk along the narrow path, for this alone led to the glorious life which was to cheer and save the world. When he talks to men about the two ways, one of them narrow and the other one broad, he is speaking out of his own experience; and when he urges men to choose the narrow one in preference to the one which is broad, he is only saying, "Follow me!"

One Way

In the realm of the intellect he chose the way which was narrow. There is a feeling now prevalent that it is unwise for a man to confine himself to any one religion or any one particular statement of belief. It is better—so men say—not to pin your faith to the sleeve of any one idea or truth, but hold yourself in readiness to accept every idea which may come your way. Keep the windows and doors of your mind wide open and let everything blow through which the winds may be able to catch up, but do not settle down upon any definite conceptions of God or the soul, of duty or destiny, because in so doing you narrow yourself and may ultimately degenerate into a bigot. With this sort of philosophy Jesus of Nazareth had no sympathy. To him certain conceptions of God were true and others were false; certain estimates of man were correct and others erroneous; certain standards of duty were uplifting and others degrading; and with all his mind and soul and strength he clung to the true and combated the false.

He never shrank from holding clean-cut opinions and from expressing them with vigor and emphasis. He was not afraid of being called intolerant or a bigot. He made a distinction between falsehood and truth, and was not ashamed to stamp upon the former and proclaim boldly the latter. Errors he struck no matter who held them, and hallucinations he repudiated no matter by how many accepted. In many a modern circle he would have been counted a narrow man, for he made no compromises, and he would not bend, and he maintained with unflinching persistency the things which his heart knew to be true and good.

He swept other leaders and teachers out of the way with gorgeous sweeps of scorn. "Other men," he said, "have taught you this or that, but I say unto you...." And when his hearers, amazed by the boldness of his speech, lifted their eyes, they saw that he had placed himself above even Moses and the prophets. He would not allow his followers to roam at their will through the realms of thought, accepting everything or nothing at their own whim or fancy; but he taught them day after day certain definite and positive conceptions and principles to which they must cling or else lose their souls. He came to bear witness to the truth, and for that reason he was not broad enough to give a place in his heart to falsehood.

Right and Wrong

This same narrowness comes out again in the limited range of things he approved. There were some things he could praise, and there were other things he was obliged to condemn. There were some men he could eulogize, and there were other men fit for nothing but burning condemnation. He did not wear a universal smile. He did not group men together as though they were all alike. He made distinctions, and he taught other men to make them too. There is a weak and sentimental way of lumping men together and trying to make it appear that men are all substantially alike and that one is not so much better after all than another. Jesus' estimate was the product of a severe discrimination. He had eyes which saw through the exterior of men's hearts, and he judged them with a fearlessness which made them crouch in terror.

The gang of thieves who carried on their business in the temple were driven out in bewilderment and consternation. To some of the most influential men of Jerusalem he said, "You are fools and blind men; you are serpents; you are vipers!" Between some men and other men there was a great gulf fixed. He did not minimize the heinousness of sin by treating all men alike. It makes no difference to some of us whether men are honest or not, or whether they live filthy lives or not; but it made a difference to Jesus. No mean and contemptible scoundrel ever felt in Jesus' presence like holding up his head. He was so narrow in his judgments that he refused to let bad men feel that they were good. In all his judgments on the lives of men, he pursued the narrow way.

It is in his habit of drawing distinctions and setting boundaries that we are to find the cause of many things which might otherwise remain inexplicable. One of the notes of Jesus' life was joy. He was a man acquainted with grief, and yet his joy was without measure. It was one of the things he had so much of that he could bequeath it to his disciples. Could he have been happy had he not walked within narrow limits? What period in any man's life is so wretched as that which lies in the later teens or early twenties in which he does not know what he is going to do? The big wide world lies stretched out before him with uncounted possibilities, and the young man full of vigor and ambition, capable of doing a hundred different things, is wretched. There are a hundred doors which he can open, but he does not know which one to try. There are a hundred fields in which he can expend his strength, but he cannot decide which field to enter. There are a hundred enterprises he feels sure he could lead to victory, but he cannot decide which one is most worthy of his leadership. And of all mortals such a youth is most miserable. No man can be happy with an entire world to roam over.

One Focus

It is only when a man picks out some particular little sphere and says, "Inside of this I purpose to work," that real life begins and his heart learns the art of singing. So long as the world's work lies in a mountain mass, there is only depression and hopelessness; it is when a man picks up in his hand a definite, tiny task and says, "This is the thing to which I shall devote my life," that the shadows vanish and life becomes worth living. It is the narrow path that leads to life.

Jesus' work was definite. At twelve he knew the business to which he must give himself. There never was a day on which he allowed himself to be inveigled into doing something else. Right here is where we are prone to blunder, and it is at this point that we should look for the root cause of much of the disquiet in our souls. We start out to do a certain work and immediately people begin to say: "Why don't you do this?" "Come and do this!" and before we are aware of our folly, we have dissipated our energy in trying to do things which God never intended us to attempt. It is here that we blunder in our benevolences. We try to give to many causes, and the result is we have little joy in our giving. It is no man's duty to contribute to every good cause that passes his way, and it is only when we draw a circle around our beneficence that we become what God likes to see—a cheerful giver. If you want to see a man who sings at his work, look for him inside of a narrow circle.

The Power of Focus

Not only was Jesus joyful, but he was mighty. He made an impression because he stayed in one place, and hit the same nail on the head until it was driven completely in. Had he wandered over the earth speaking his parables, they would have fallen into more ears but would have molded fewer hearts. By staying in Palestine and keeping his heart close to a few chosen hearts, he became increasingly influential so that the authorities were frightened, fearing that he might overturn the nation. The men who were the nearest to him became so passionately in love with him that they were ready to die for him. He made himself thus mighty by limiting himself. It is with men as it is with rivers: a river becomes a river only by the assistance of its banks. The difference between a river and a swamp is that a river has banks and a swamp has none. Similarly, it is when our life, by some sorrow or calamity or fresh responsibilities, is compressed within a narrower channel that it takes on interior richness and gains a significance which it never had before.

By limiting himself our Lord came off conqueror. He succeeded. What is it to succeed? It is to do the thing for which we were created. The most galling of all experiences is the failure to do that which is most worthwhile. Jesus attempted to do one thing only, and that was to perform the work which his Father had given him to do. At the end of his life he could look into his Father's face and say, "I have finished the work which you gave me to do." It was indeed time that the Father should glorify the Son! Jesus' life on earth covered only thirty-three brief years, and yet he did the greatest piece of work ever accomplished on the earth. It is wonderful what a stupendous task can be accomplished in a little time if a man is only willing to keep at it.

'Follow Me'

We have been touching upon a great principle—the principle which lies at the basis of all the fine arts. The arts which are called "fine" become fine because of the narrowness of the limitations which they impose. They all subject the soul to a discipline which is severe and insist upon a bondage which cannot be broken through. In music there is no leeway left to the singer. He cannot sing a little sharp or a little flat and still produce music. In music everything is precise, exact, severe, and all the tones must take accurately the precise points assigned them by the master, else the music does not have in it that indescribable power which lifts and entrances the soul. The artist cannot dip his brush as he pleases into this color or that, careless as to how much of this or how little of that he spreads on the canvas. He is held in the grip of laws which he cannot violate even a little without marring the picture. It is the narrow way on which artists must forever walk.

But the most difficult of all the fine arts is the high art of living as God would have a mortal to live. Singing is easy—and so is painting—compared with this exacting, soul-taxing art of living. One cannot think anything he pleases, or feel as he wants to, or act as he is inclined to. He must walk the narrow path. Jesus walked it, and he calls men everywhere to become his followers. He is rigorous in his demands. He is inexorable in his commands. He is clear and firm in the limitations which he imposes. He says, "Come to me!" We ask, "Cannot we go to others?" His reply is, "There are not others. Come to me!" And when we come, he says, "Follow me!" We hesitate and ask, "Is this really necessary? Can we not choose an easier way?!" His reply is: "Follow me." "If you do not take up your cross and follow me, you cannot be my disciple, and no one comes to the Father except through me." He says, "Abide in me!" and we demur and wonder if after all it is necessary to shut ourselves up in what seems to be so narrow and limited a sphere. But he says to us with that strange, definite, compelling accent which stirred the hearts of the people long ago in Galilee, "Verily I say unto you, unless you abide in me, you have no life at all in you!"

This, then, is the narrowness of Jesus. He is narrow for a purpose. He limited himself, emptied himself of his divine glory, was found in the fashion of a man, walked the narrow path which led from the carpenter's shop to Golgotha, all because of his great love for us, and in order that we might each one of us have life and have it more abundantly.

THE BREADTH
OF JESUS

There is a sense in which Jesus of Nazareth was lacking in breadth. He had apparently no desire to see the world and was content to spend his life in little Palestine. He walked a path which was narrow and refused to give his approval to men and measures which won the esteem and praise of thousands of his countrymen. But there was a purpose in this narrowness and a reason for it. His narrowness was a product of his breadth.

He walked the narrow path because he carried in his heart the dream of an empire which was vast. By standing in one place and striking repeatedly the strings of the same set of hearts, he started vibrations which have filled the world with music. By carefully tending the fire which he had kindled, he made it hot enough to change the spiritual climate of many lands. By saturating a little circle of chosen followers with his spirit, he made them capable of carrying on their shoulders a lost race to God.

By persistently treading a single path, he made that path so luminous that every eye can see it: By discarding false ideas and by opposing wicked men, he has made it easier for truth seekers and the

77

soldiers of God in each succeeding generation to fight a good fight and to win the crown. By being faithful in a few things, he won the place of Lordship over many cities; and by limiting himself, by making himself of no reputation, he founded a kingdom broad as humanity and of which there shall be no end. If you study the New Testament, you will see that this man, from the beginning, carried the world in his eye and the race on his heart. What strange paradoxes one finds in the realm of the soul. If you would be broad, then be narrow. Jesus was narrow because his breadth was immeasurable.

Breadth Brings Conflict

It was the breadth of Jesus' ideas and sympathies which first brought him into conflict with his countrymen. The Jews, as a people, were proverbially narrow and bigoted. They divided the world into two parts and placed an almost impassable gulf between themselves and all other races. Inside of Palestine people were divided into classes by lines which were straight and unchangeable. Hearts were narrow, and feelings were bitter and hard. Samaria was counted accursed, and men of Galilee on their way to Jerusalem crossed over the Jordan in order that their feet might not be contaminated by treading the Samaritan soil. The Jews were an exclusive and haughty and aristocratic race, constantly thanking God that they were superior to all other nations.

But the spirit of Jesus was different. In his very first sermon in Nazareth he called attention to the fact that in the days of Elijah, God had picked a widow outside of the promised land for special consideration and honor and that in the days of Elisha, although there were many lepers in Israel, God had passed by them all and healed a Gentile leper, Naaman the Syrian. It was all written down in their Scriptures, but the good people in Nazareth, like many other good people since their day, did not pay attention to many things written in their own Scriptures. And when Jesus began to eulogize the widow of Sidon and the Syrian king, their hearts became so hot within them that they broke up the meeting and tried to mob the preacher. This is really the beginning of Jesus' conflict with the world. The narrow-headed villagers of Nazareth were driven to the edge of murder by the breadth of a mind which went beyond them.

Broad Enough for All Ages

The amplitude of Jesus' ideas is evidenced by their perennial freshness and applicability to all kinds of men and conditions. How wonderful it is that Jesus' ideas are broad enough to cover all the nations and all the centuries. Many ideas shrivel and dry up with the lapse of time. Political ideas have a strange fashion of passing away, and so do scientific ideas. One century has no interest in the political teachings of the century which preceded it, and no generation is willing to accept the science of the generation that went before it. But the ideas of Jesus have such breadth that they can cover the world and the ages. Although nineteen centuries have swept away almost everything which was believed and taught in Jesus' day, his ideas are still alive and the very words in which they are expressed are destined to outlive the stars.

This is indeed strange, that we people of the twentieth century should be a part of the Nazareth congregation, listening to the very ideas which interested Jews nearly two thousand years ago. So broad are these ideas and so universally applicable to the demands of the mind and the needs of the heart that each succeeding generation down to the end of time will take its place in the congregation of the prophet of Nazareth. If we could see the whole history unrolled before him, we would discover the countless millions of humanity gathered round a single teacher—none other than the teacher whom the people of Nazareth tried to kill. Broad, indeed, must be the ideas which can cover all peoples and kindreds and tongues throughout all the eras of their existence.

And his heart was as far-reaching as his brain. The social sympathies of Jesus were, to his countrymen, a surprise and a scandal. He felt with everybody. He seemed to be ignorant of the proprieties and the etiquette of well-bred people. His heart went out to all sorts and conditions of men in a way which was reckless and shocking.

There were men in Palestine who were under the ban of public opinion. Every right-thinking man despised them. They were treated like the dogs in the street. They had feelings, but nobody felt with them. Every door of society was slammed in their face. These men were known as Publicans [tax collectors]. Jesus' heart went out to these men. He talked with them, ate with them. Not content with this, he took one of them into the inner circle of his intimate friends and allowed him to go out and teach and work in his name. Even in Jericho, the narrowest of all Judean cities because for centuries it had been the home of the priests, this big-hearted prophet took dinner with one of the most notorious of all the Publicans—to the consternation of the best people in the land. And not content with thus showing the breadth of his sympathies by his deeds, he painted a picture recorded in Scripture whose colors will never fade, and no thief can ever destroy it. It is the picture entitled "The Pharisee and the Publican," which shows that God's heart is more responsive to a penitent Publican than to a vainglorious Pharisee.

> **By carefully tending the fire which he had kindled, he made it hot enough to change the spiritual climate of many lands.**

There was only one set of men lower than the Publicans, and they were the Samaritans. Every man's hand was against them. Every heart was hard as flint toward them. And Jesus befriended them. He felt with them. He gave religious instruction even to a Samaritan woman and healed even a Samaritan leper. So wide was his heart that there was room in it for a Samaritan outcast whose flesh was rotten. And, as if determined that all the world down to the end of time should know the width of his sympathies, he painted a picture which men will look at as long as they have eyes to see and hearts to feel, and the name of the picture is "The Good Samaritan."

What havoc this man made with the traditions and customs of his countrymen! The land was crossed in all directions by dividing walls and estranging barriers, constructed by narrow-hearted teachers, and after Jesus had walked through the land, lo, the barriers and walls were a mass of ruins! His great, loving heart burst asunder all the regulations and restrictions. There was room in his soul for everybody.

Loving Enough to Forgive

It is the width of his love that men have found most to wonder at. His love was unbounded. It was an ocean without a shore. He was not willing that his followers should set boundaries to their love, because all such barriers were contrary to his habit and foreign to his spirit. When Peter asked him how often a man ought to forgive another who has trespassed against him, and suggested seven as a number almost grotesquely large, being more than twice the number suggested by the most liberal of the rabbis, Jesus [in essence] said: "Do not set any limits at all. There are no boundaries in the realm of love. You cannot calculate in the empire of the heart. Mathematics is foreign to affection."

Whenever he spoke about love, he said something which amazed his hearers. One day he said, "Love your enemies; bless them that curse you; do good to them that hate you; and pray for them that despitefully use you and persecute you" [Matthew 5:44 KJV]. And when men stood aghast, showing by their faces that only God could be expected to have a love so broad, Jesus went on to add that God is to be the model of all men who want to live right and that their constant aim shall be to bring their lives up to God's style and to imitate Him in the unbounded reach of His good will. Nor was this simply exhortation—it was not only preaching, but practice.

Jesus taught forgiveness because he knew the blessedness of a forgiving heart. He himself was forgiving always. He had no grudges, no retaliations, no revenges. Jesus saw the loathsomeness of vice, knew the odiousness of vulgarity, felt the hideousness of sin. His heart was so sensitive that it blazed against evil, but while he loathed the sin, he could love the sinner; and so when his executioners nailed his hands and feet to the cross, the only word which escaped his lips was, "Forgive," "Forgive," "Forgive." That great word contained the blood of his heart.

Unfettered Hope

It is this abounding love which accounts for the immeasurable reaches of his hope. He was the most hopeful of all teachers. No matter how dull the pupil, he still believed that he would learn. Men had grown cynical and pessimistic in Palestine nineteen centuries ago. They had lost confidence in humanity, and had settled down in the conviction that for many mortals we can expect nothing but damnation.

To the religious teachers of Palestine certain classes were beyond redemption. It was known throughout the city that to certain sinners no exhortation could be directed, no promise could be offered. The Jewish church turned its back upon all such and confined itself to men who could be saved. But Jesus, because he loved, also hoped. His hope was as immeasurable as his love. He did not reject the refuse of society. He saw promise even in the scum. The dregs of society are not to be carelessly tossed away. There is a chance for the man who is supposed to have no chance, there is hope for the man whom men have doomed to destruction.

You cannot tell what is in a man by what he says—or even by what he does. There is more in him than comes out in his words and his deeds. And so Jesus proceeded to show that the so-called lost men were not lost and that, even in Samaria, the fields were white to the harvest. He did not hesitate to direct his most earnest exhortations to men who were supposed to have no heart, and even when the world's cruelty was cutting into him like steel, he said, "I, if I be lifted up, will draw all men unto me" [John 12:32 KJV]. So boundless was his confidence in man that he set no limits on his expectations.

The Method of Jesus

If you were going to form an organization for the purpose of carrying out your ideas after your death, what kind of men would you select? You would—I suspect—choose men like yourself, of your own social circle, your own type of mind, your own general temperament and make-up, and in so doing, you would have a society which would come to nothing. Mark the method of Jesus.

He chooses men of all grades and from all classes. No man in the group is like any of his comrades, and no one of them is like Jesus. There is a mercurial man, Peter; and there is a lymphatic man, Thomas. There is a fire-eater, Simon Zelotes, a member of the fieriest political party in Palestine; and there is the prosaic and slow-going Philip. There is a man of good family and spotless reputation, John; and by his side is a man with a tarnished name, Matthew, the Publican. All temperaments are here and all combinations of mental faculties; and here are representatives from various classes and differing social strata. In doing a wide work you must have a broad instrument, and the Christian church, as it left the hands of Jesus, embraced in its membership the types of men which would be able to open all the doors.

Never does the breadth of the mind of Jesus come out with more startling clearness than in the manner of his choices in the formation of the society which was to bear his name and carry on his work. It was a great work, the vastest which has ever entered into the heart of man. He had constantly the ends of the earth in his eye. The narrowness of the petty men who administered the affairs of the Jewish church distressed him. "Many," he said, "shall come from the East and the West and from the North and the South and shall sit down with Abraham and Isaac and Jacob in the Kingdom of God" [Matthew 8:11 KJV].

At an early stage he told his apostles not to go outside the limits of their own people in their work, but this limitation of field was only educational and, with their increasing strength, was to pass forever away. Men should stay in Jerusalem long enough to secure strength sufficient to grapple with problems of Judea; and they should tarry in Judea until they were capable of grappling with the more difficult conditions of Samaria; and they should work in Samaria until they had acquired the endurance which would enable them to travel to the uttermost parts of the earth.

In the earlier stages a teacher does not communicate to the pupil his plans for the years which lie far ahead. Jesus did not talk to his apostles about the world and the ages on the day of their baptism, or even in the upper chamber, but right before he left the earth, he poured into their ear the great message which had been in his heart from the beginning, and it ran thus, "Go preach the Gospel to the whole creation." All national boundaries are now obliterated, and the horizon thrown round the apostles is not less narrow than the large circle of the world. "Go disciple the nations." It was in this manner that he spoke to them before the cloud took him from their sight, and whenever, from that day to this, the followers of Jesus have been closest to him, they have been found to be dreaming of conquests wide as the world.

Whoever you are, and wherever you are, and whatever you are, you are included in His plans [of discipling the nations]. When He laid down the lines of His vast scheme for humanity, you were not overlooked or forgotten. When He framed His church, a place inside of it was assigned to you. That place will remain vacant until you fill it. You cannot escape Him. His arms are all-embracing. The width of His heart is infinite. His love is everlasting.

"He trusted on God."
MATTHEW 27:43 KJV

JESUS' TRUST IN GOD

We are trying to see Jesus as he was. It is surprising that we do not know him better when his image is so vividly portrayed for us in the Gospels. The very familiarity of the story has a deadening effect upon the mind. We have heard so much of Jesus ever since the days of childhood, have heard so many teachers and preachers speak about him, that the mind has hardened and refuses to be impressed by him.

Many of us have had faulty methods of Bible study. We have studied the Bible piecemeal, in scraps and patches, getting a knowledge of isolated passages and never putting together the various parts so as to see Jesus as a man among men. We have caught, it may be, one trait of his lovely character; we have fixed our gaze upon one bright particular star and have missed the sweep and swing of the constellations; we have picked up a pebble now and then and have failed to take in the curve of the vast shore and the swell and surge of the sea. Our object in all these studies is to see him as he was seen by the men of his time.

We have already found in him the note of strength and the note of gladness, and now let us get a little deeper and find out, if we can, the spring from which strength and gladness flow. How does it happen that this man was so masterful in every situation, and how did it come to pass that he was joyful in the midst of so many shadows? The answer to the question lies written broad on all the pages of the New Testament.

From Beginning to End

Jesus' strength and gladness came from his steadfast trust in God. If you were to ask me what is deepest and most fundamental in the character of Jesus, I should say that it was his trust in God. I see not how anyone can read the New Testament without feeling that this to him was the Alpha and the Omega, the first and the last. It was the heaven above his head, the earth beneath his feet, the atmosphere he daily breathed, the spirit in which he was saturated, the music that ran through all his conversation, the inspiration of all his life.

Possibly no better testimony upon this point can be found in all the Scriptures than that taken from the lips of his deadliest foes. We have already found these enemies of Jesus to be valuable witnesses, and they will not disappoint us here. When he was dying on the cross, many people laughed at him and wagged their heads, saying derisive and spiteful things. Among these people, strange to say, there were members of the Sanhedrin, chief priests, Scribes and leaders— they all ridiculed and scorned him, and the climax of their vituperation was this, "He trusted on God!" [Matthew 27:43 kjv]. No uglier jeer ever was belched forth from the jaws of hell than that. It is incredible that human beings could be so diabolical as to sneer at a man in the hour of death, but that is what the religious leaders of Palestine did when the Prophet of Galilee was dying. The dark and terrible sentence throws a blaze of light upon the teaching and the conduct of Jesus. His whole course of action had made upon the people among whom he moved the impression that he trusted in God.

Should you ask me for illustrations of this trust, I should be embarrassed, not because there are so few, but because there are so many. One can dip into the Gospels where he will and find things which bear testimony to Jesus' trust in God. When only a boy he said to his mother, "Why were you searching for me? Didn't you know I had to be in my Father's house?" [Luke 2:49 NIV].

His last words upon the cross were, "Father, into your hands I commend my spirit" [Luke 23:46 KJV]. From that first point to the last point, the music of his trust was never broken.

Unceasing Prayer

Jesus is everywhere and always a man of prayer. At the crises of his life we find him praying. At his baptism and the transfiguration, in the Garden and on the cross, he is pouring out his soul to God. Before every important action, in the midst of every difficult situation, at the completion of every stage of work, we find him praying. It was a common thing in Palestine for men to pray, but no man had ever prayed like this man, with such simplicity, with such earnestness, with such boundless trust.

Men gathered round him awestruck and said, "Master, teach us how to pray." All Hebrew children were taught to pray from earliest infancy. Prayer was an indispensable feature of Hebrew piety, but men who had prayed from earliest youth felt, when they heard this man pray, that they had never prayed at all. The word which he applied to God was "Father." Only occasionally in the long sweep of the ages had a soul here and there ventured to apply to Deity a name so familiar and sweet, but Jesus of Nazareth always thinks and speaks of God as Father. He names Him this in his own prayers, he tells other men that they also may use this name. To trust in the goodness and mercy of the good Father was his own intensest and fullest delight; to induce others to trust in Him also was his constant ambition and endeavor.

Trouble with Our Trust

How much Jesus has to teach us at this point. It is often supposed that it is easy to believe in God. The fact is, nothing is more difficult to do at certain times and in certain circumstances. It is easy, indeed, to say that one trusts in God, but really to do it when justice seems dead and love seems to have vanished, that is difficult indeed. Who can study Nature without finding things in it which make it difficult to believe in the good Father? Does not Nature seem to be cruel? Does she seem to have any heart? Do not fires burn and waters drown and volcanoes cover cities without mercy? Does Nature not carry on her vast operations with absolute indifference to the wishes or welfare of men? All of the great thinkers who have gazed into the face of Nature have been appalled by her heartlessness and her indifference.

Jesus of Nazareth found in Nature fresh evidences of God's love. Other men, noting how the sunshine falls upon the heads of the good and the bad, come to the conclusion that God does not know—God does not care. Whereas Jesus, looking on the same phenomenon, sees in it fresh evidence of the great heart of the good Father. The rain falls upon the farm of the man who blasphemes and also upon the farm of the man who serves God, not because God is indifferent to the difference in character, but because he is so good that his mercy covers all of his children. Just as the earthly parent allows the disobedient son to sit down at the table with his obedient brothers and sisters, so it is the good God who feeds the good and the bad, the just and the unjust, unwilling to show resentment, hoping still that every heart will surrender. To Jesus, Nature is a great witness, clothed in light, bearing continuous testimony to the width of the eternal mercy.

> If you were to ask me what is deepest and most fundamental in the character of Jesus, I should say that it was his trust in God.

But if Nature seems indifferent and cruel, what shall we say of history—the arena in which has been played out the tragedy of human life? What a jumble of mysteries! What a mass of woes! All the centuries groaning with agony, all of the ages dripping with blood! Who can look upon the sufferings of the innocent, or hear the cries of the oppressed, or witness the slaughter of the pure and the good without asking himself: Does God know? Does God care? Right forever on the scaffold, wrong forever on the throne—so it seems to the man who reads history. Vice triumphs over virtue, dishonesty tramples upon honesty, injustice lords it over justice, hate defies and defeats love. This happens not once but ten thousand times. Some men read the dark and terrible story and give up their faith in God.

Jesus looks upon the same scene and gives to it a different interpretation. He sees good men come and offer their services to the world only to be rejected and repulsed. One of them is stoned; another is beaten; another is killed. Their dead bodies are piled up in sickening heaps, but to Jesus this is not evidence of the indifference of God—it is the proof of his long-suffering patience; it is because he is not willing that any should be lost that he keeps on century after century, sending into the world prophets and apostles, heroes and saints, who shall proclaim the message of heaven to bewildered and sinful man.

Trusting Through Tribulations

But if the processes of Nature and the courses of history make war upon one's trust in God, much more terrible is the conflict which is often necessitated by one's own personal experience. Many a man has for years trusted in God only to discover when evil fortune came that his trust was not strong enough to stand the shock. The very best and strongest of men, when overtaken by misfortune, are obliged to readjust their faith. For a while they are stupefied and dazed, scarcely knowing where to turn or what to think.

Many things conspire to blot out one's trust in God. Disappointment may do it; a man's fondest dream may come to nothing; his central ambition may fail. One disappointment after another may come upon him until he sinks down, vanquished and hopeless, his torch extinguished. Persecution may break a man's faith in God; the inhumanity of man may turn sour the juices of the heart; the misunderstandings and misrepresentations of men, their hostility and faithlessness, their contempt and their scorn, may render it well-nigh impossible to believe that God rules the world.

Other men are overcome by failure. Nothing to them was so sweet as success. To win success they give the best of their years and all their powers, but, in spite of all they can do, success does not come. At the end of the day they confess themselves defeated. In the bitterness of their defeat they cry out, "Where is God?"

Impeccable Trust

Jesus of Nazareth had all the dark experiences which it is possible for the soul to have. He had a work to do to which he gave all the energy of his brain and his heart. He had a dream which filled him with enthusiasm; he had a message to communicate which he was certain would drive away the gloom and the woe of the world. He went to Jerusalem to announce it—the door there was slammed in his face. He announced it in the synagogues of Galilee, but the people there would not receive it. He then preached it on the street corners of a great city, but the crowds melted away like snow banks in June. There were, in the end, only twelve men who stood by him, and the hearts of these were so fluctuating that he said, "You do not want to leave too, do you?" [John 6:67 NIV]. To these twelve men he gave himself with passionate devotion, pouring into their souls his own very life. But the boldest of them turned out a coward, and one of the most trusted of them became a traitor, and when the crisis in his life came, they all forsook him and fled.

But despite his disappointment, his trust in God was unbroken. In the midst of the tempest his torch kept on burning, and he cried, "Be of good cheer, I have overcome the world" [John 16:33 KJV]. He was maligned, abused, denounced. He was accused of blasphemy, of treason, but his heart remained sweet. Men buffeted him and abused him, hissing at him their ingratitude and hatred, but he said, "The cup which my Father has given me to drink, shall I not drink it?"

We dwell upon the things which have happened since his death, and dwelling upon these, we see that he has succeeded; but it should never be forgotten that his life on the day of his death [appeared to be] a terrible and heart-breaking failure. Injustice was stronger than justice; unrighteousness was mightier than righteousness; hate was stronger than love. He had tried to induce the world to accept a beautiful truth, but the world spurned him. In the hour of his great defeat he still looked to God saying, "Not my will but thine be done" [Luke 22:42 KJV]. Defeat itself could not daunt him or make him draw back. "If it is necessary," he [in essence] said, "that I should be sacrificed, that I should be trodden under the feet of the men who are thirsting for my blood, if that is the will of the Infinite Father, then to that I gladly submit."

Never was there a man like this man. Other great and strong men have lived and labored, but never a man like Jesus of Nazareth. In the midst of the wildest storm that ever blotted out the heavens and caused the earth to quake, he looked steadily toward God, saying, "Not my will but thine be done" [Luke 22:42 KJV]. Look down across the ages and see the great men, how they are swayed and tossed by the winds and storms; but there above them all rises this man of Galilee like some majestic mountain.

"First be reconciled to thy brother."
MATTHEW 5:24 KJV

THE BROTHERLINESS OF JESUS

We have found that the secret of his joy and strength lay in his implicit trust in God, and now I wish to think with you about another trait for which it is difficult for me to find a satisfying name.

I should say that it is the love of Jesus were not the word "love" so ambiguous and so liable to misinterpretation; I should say it was the service of Jesus were it not for the fact that "service" is rather cold and has long since been worn into shreds; I should say the "pity" of Jesus, but pity is love looking downward, and that does not convey all the truth; I should say the kindness of Jesus, but the word does not carry with it force enough. Possibly we cannot do better than to take the word "brotherliness," for this word contains two elements, both of which are essential if we would understand the kind of man Jesus was. Brotherliness carries in it not only a sense of kinship, but likewise a disposition to render help. There is a relationship, and likewise a helpfulness, and both of these blended into one constitute the quality to which I invite your attention now.

Even His Critics

That this trait in Jesus made a profound impression upon his contemporaries is evidenced not only by what his friends have said about him, but also by the criticisms and sneers which he drew from his foes. It was a common taunt of the Scribes and Pharisees that he was a friend of Publicans and sinners, and when he hung dying on the cross, the leading men of the Jewish church gathered round him saying with a jeer, "He saved others; He cannot save Himself" [Mark 15:31 NASB]. Both of these accusations are as devilish as anything to be found in the literature of the world, but they are valuable to us in this: They show conclusively what impression this man of Galilee made upon the people of his time.

It had been his practice all the way through life to help men. He had been a friendly, brotherly man, even to the lowest and the basest members of society. That was a characteristic which had created a great scandal and made him hateful to many of the respectable people of his day. The same trait is characterized in a famous phrase written by one of his dearest friends, "He went about doing good." What more beautiful eulogy has ever been written about a man than that? In these three sentences—"The friend of Publicans and sinners;" "He saved others; he cannot save himself;" and "He went about doing good"—we get eloquent testimony to the fact that Jesus had a brotherly heart.

Let us look into the accusation that he was the friend of Publicans and sinners and find out what it meant. The word "Publican" means nothing to us because we have no class of men corresponding to the Publicans of Palestine. They were the Jewish tax-gatherers for the Roman government. They were the hirelings of great capitalists into whose hands it was necessary to turn over a certain sum of money each year, and by extortion and other dishonest measures, they could make just as much money for themselves.

To every pious Hebrew these men were traitors to their country, and wherever they went, they were an object of abhorrence, hatred and scorn. Their money was tainted money; it would not be accepted in the synagogue. Their oath was absolutely worthless. They could not be a witness in any court of law. If a man promised to do a thing for a Publican under oath, he was not bound to keep his oath. They were set up in the pillory of scorn and denunciation, and pelted with sneers by every passer-by. They were looked upon as wild beasts in human shape. They were outcasts, vagabonds, worse than the homeless curs that roamed the streets. No decent man would have anything to do with them; no religious teacher took any interest in them. They were simply the offscouring and dregs of society.

But even with these, Jesus made friends. Not only did he speak to them, but he ate with them, went into their houses and sat down to the table with them! It is one thing to throw money to depraved men as we would throw carrots to bears in a bear pit; it is another thing to eat with them. It is one thing to talk down to bad men, giving them good advice, and quite another thing to associate with them. But this man Jesus sat down and ate with Publicans; he crossed the chasm over which no man of his day or generation was willing to cross. By doing this he lost his reputation. In the words of an apostle he made himself of no reputation [Philippians 2:7 KJV]; he took his good name and tore it into shreds and threw it away—all because he was determined to be brotherly. Although these men were so base, he recognized in them his brothers. They belonged to him, and he belonged to them. They were members of the human race, children of the great family of God and therefore, in spite of all that they had done and regardless of all that

> They were bound round and round with laws, like an Egyptian mummy with embalming cloths, but Jesus gave himself to the work of setting them free.

they were, he treated them as brothers. Not only did this conduct make a profound impression upon the men of Jesus' day, but it has made such a deep impression on all succeeding generations that it has blinded us to a fact that should never be forgotten: Jesus was the brother of everybody.

Loving the Wealthy, Too

Christianity has often been conceived as a religion that is interested chiefly in the outcasts of society, in the poor, the sick, the depraved. There are many who always think of Jesus as the friend of poor men, and of sick men, and of bad men, who never think of him as the brother of those that are rich and strong and good. It should never be forgotten that Jesus was brotherly toward good men as well as bad men, rich men as well as poor men, respectable men as well as disreputable men—he was the brother of every man. If more is said in the New Testament about poor men than rich men, it is because Jesus was able to come nearer to poor men than he was to rich men. Rich men are always inaccessible. Here in New York you can go into the homes of the poor anywhere, but from the homes of the rich you are barred out. Rich men always surround themselves with barriers, with cordons of servants and therefore, we must not be surprised that in Palestine it was necessary for this man of Galilee to deal largely with the poor.

But it must not be forgotten that he was just as friendly toward the rich Nicodemus as he was to the poor woman at the well and that he was just as brotherly toward rich Zaccheus as he was to the poor beggar in Jerusalem. Nor was he lacking in brotherly interest in the respectable people of his day. If the New Testament makes the impression on us that he was more interested in the outcast and debased, it is because this interest in them was so exceptional that it made a greater impression upon those who wrote the story of his life than any other feature of his conduct.

The pious Hebrews of Palestine were tied hand and foot with the cords of tradition. They were bound round and round with laws, like an Egyptian mummy with embalming cloths, but Jesus gave himself to the work of setting them free. The cords were tied tight, and he attempted to untie the knots. But in his effort to give men emancipation, he stirred up animosities and awakened hatred which led speedily to his death. It was in his effort to untie the knots that men seized him, crying, "Crucify him!"

'Like His Brothers in Every Way'

Let us notice a few illustrations of his brotherliness. When John the Baptist was baptizing in the Jordan, Jesus came down from Galilee to be baptized. John, when he saw Jesus approaching, cried out: "O, no, I cannot baptize you, you are too good. There is reason why I should be baptized of you. This baptism is intended for sinners. I will not, therefore, baptize you." But Jesus would not listen to him; he insisted upon being baptized. He would identify himself with his brethren. "I want to be counted," he said, "a man among men." It was not a question of whether he was good or not; it was a question of being brotherly. He refused to remain aloof from any movement that promised good to his country. He subjected himself to the same action of which his fellow-citizens were in need. He took his place at the very beginning of his ministry among his brethren.

Radical Teachings

His brotherliness is also manifested in his teaching. He could not look into men's faces without being pained by their confusion, their perplexity and their misery. He could not see men passing on to the Judgment Day without telling them something about the great God in whose world they were living. Whenever he saw men fainting and scattered abroad like sheep having no shepherd, his heart was moved with compassion on them. When he looked into the tired faces of the Galilean peasants, his heart cried out, "Come to me all you who are weary and burdened, and I will give you rest" [Matthew 11:28 NIV]. What a sob there is in the words, "O Jerusalem! Jerusalem!" [Luke 13:34 KJV]. There is in the words the moan of a brotherly heart. And not only was he brotherly himself, but to him brotherliness is the very essence of religion. Without brotherliness there can be no religion that is pleasing unto God.

The old law had said that one man must not kill another, but Jesus went far beyond the requirements of that law. He said that calling a man names was also wicked and would bring him into judgment. To use adjectives that pierce and cut, to throw out mean epithets full of haughtiness and scorn, to speak of men in ways that degrade them—this is wickedness and will bring the severest retribution.

One of the greatest of his parables is the parable of Dives and Lazarus. A rich man fares sumptuously every day, and at his gate there lies a poor sick beggar, his body covered with ulcers, with no friend to bring relief. Only the dogs that prowl the streets lick the loathsome man's sores. Jesus says when that thing happens in this world, something happens in the next world. You can almost feel the heat of his indignant soul. You can hear him asking, "Do you suppose that inhumanity like that will go unpunished in the universe of God?" It was not because the rich man was dressed in fine raiment and fared sumptuously every day that later on he lifted up his eyes in torment. Abraham also was rich and fared sumptuously every day, but Abraham went to heaven because he had a brother's heart. This rich man went to hell because his heart was not tender; his sympathy did not go out to a brother's need.

A Brother to the End

And how did Palestine receive this brotherliness? It did not like it. Jesus was too brotherly; men misunderstood him. They misinterpreted him; they maligned him; they laid their plans to kill him; but they could not make him anything else than brotherly. In spite of all their ugliness and vindictiveness, he went on helping them all he could, and when they laid their plots to kill him, he went bravely forward giving help, saying, "If I cannot help them with my life, I will help them with my death. By dying I will convince them that I wanted to do them good. I, if I be lifted up, will draw all men unto me. When hanging on the cross, they will understand me as they cannot understand me now. When they hear me praying for them with my dying breath, they will be convinced that I am indeed their brother."

"Be of good cheer."
JOHN 16:33 KJV

THE OPTIMISM OF JESUS

By optimism I do not mean that jaunty, brainless, happy-go-lucky buoyancy which so often calls itself by this pretentious name. If you insist upon defining an optimist as a man who plays only with sunbeams, and who can hear nothing but harmonies, and who is only slightly concerned with the world's agonies and tragedies because of his fancy that no matter what he or anyone else does, everything is certain to come out all right, then Jesus was not an optimist. There is a sentimental optimism which is irrational and immoral. It is the product of a shallow brain and a stupid heart. It shuts its eyes to all hideous facts and stops its ears to all horrible sounds, and insists that, in spite of appearances, all is well with the world. This sort of optimism faces the future with a confidence born not of courage but of moral indolence. It assumes that there is in the nature of things an irresistible tendency upward, and that irrespective of the conduct of any man or any set of men, all will be well in the end. No such optimism as this is known in the New Testament.

If we have our superficial optimists, we have also our shallow and short-sighted pessimists. There are men who have a genius for seeing shadows. Their ears are keen for discords. These men listen to the world's sighing and sobbing and agonizing until history seems a hideous nightmare and existence itself a curse. But from the grinning optimist and the hysterical pessimist, we can expect little. They have nothing to offer toward the solution of the great world problems.

Godly Optimism

Let us open our New Testament and listen to a man who, in these confused and distracting times, can give us confidence and hope. Jesus of Nazareth was not a man who could shut his eyes to the sorrow and the heartbreak of the world. Never were eyes wider open than his. He saw everything.

He saw things which the world had passed by unnoticed. He saw suffering in its every form—it tugged at his heart strings. Underneath the tragedy of suffering he saw the darker tragedy of sin and recognized as no one else the tremendous power of evil. He saw with open eyes the roads which lead to death. He knew, as no other has ever known so well, that evil must be resisted, that sin must be faced and grappled with, that it is only by struggle, suffering and death that the victory can be won. But he remained nevertheless undaunted. He saw both sides—the bright side and the dark side—and having seen both sides, his face had light on it. He sang and he also sobbed. His singing was sometimes broken by his sobbing, but he was never overwhelmed. He never surrendered; his head was always up, and his unfailing exhortation is, "Be of good cheer!" [John 16:33 KJV].

This is the dominating note of the New Testament. It comes up out of the heart of the worst tragedy which our world has known. What a sad and depressing book the New Testament ought to be considering the dismal story it has to tell! It gives us the life of one who was a man of sorrows and acquainted with grief. It portrays his sufferings through the cruel, disappointing years to his horrible death upon the cross. And yet, despite this heart-breaking story, the New Testament does not depress us or leave a shadow on the heart. It is a jubilant, exhilarating book, and the words which linger longest in the ear are, "Be of good cheer; I have overcome the world" [John 16:33 KJV]. The New Testament is a gospel, a bit of glorious news, because at the center of it there lives and works the world's greatest optimist.

Here is the optimist whom we have been looking for. This is the man who can inspire our confidence and give us hope. We need a man with open eye and open ear and open heart, a man who sees things as they are and knows the thickness of the belt of night. We cannot follow a leader who keeps crying, "Peace," when we know that there is not peace; nor can we trust a teacher who asserts that all is well, when his assertion is contradicted daily by the experience of the world. Give us a man who feels the fury of the storm and is also certain of the calm which is going to follow. Jesus is the prince of optimists—his optimism is the optimism of God Himself.

Unwavering Trust

Let us try to find the secret of Jesus' optimism. The secret is written large across the pages of the Gospel. It was a secret too good to keep—he gave it to everybody who had ears to hear. It was an abiding confidence in God. We are sure of Him—sometimes. Our faith is clouded, and it is intermittent. It floods and ebbs like the tide. Jesus never doubted. His vision was unclouded. His trust was absolute. To him God was an ever-present Father. This was his new name for God. The prophets and poets of Israel had only seldom ventured to think of God as father, and then only by way of dim surmise. With Jesus, God was always Father. This is the name he carried on his lips when a boy of twelve; it was on his lips when he passed from this world into the other. He placed it on the lips of every man who followed him. It constantly amazed him that men had so little faith in God. "Have faith in God!" [Mark 11:22 KJV]. This was the exhortation to live his life and do his work. The words came with the power of a revelation, because they were warm with the blood of a heart which knew the secret of perfect trust.

Along with unswerving trust in God, there went an unshakable confidence [that men could change]. He saw the possibilities and capacities of the human heart. He saw men's littlenesses, frailties, vices and sins, but underneath all these he saw a soul created in God's image. He called Simon, the son of Jonas, a rock, when Simon was counted the most fickle and fluctuating man in all the town. Jesus saw that which was deepest in him. He had confidence not only in people who "went to church," but also in people who never went. He had hope for the Publicans and sinners. He knew that Zaccheus could repent and that Matthew could become a preacher. He believed that men and women who have fallen all the way to the bottom can climb back again. "The harlots are going into the kingdom before you!"—thus he spoke to a company of hard-hearted pessimists.

> It was because the eyes of Jesus swept the future that he could stand around the wreckage of a race in ruins and say, "Be of good cheer!"

Nor could any experience break down this trust in the divine capacities of human nature. When has a man had greater reason to abandon faith in men than this optimist of Galilee? He lived in a corrupt and demoralizing age. Government was both tyrannical and rotten. Its officials were, for the most part, cynics and grafters. The Jewish church was formal, lifeless and hypocritical. Its leaders, many of them, were dead to the movements of God's Spirit. Society was disgustingly corrupt. Jesus himself was suspected, misrepresented, hated. He was surrounded by liars wherever he went. No matter what he said, his sentences were twisted, and no matter what he did, his motives were impugned. Such treatment is apt to sour the heart of anyone who is long subjected to it. Jesus was mistreated all the way. But he never gave up [on the fact that men could change]. When he saw that men were determined to take his life, he said, "If I be lifted up, I will draw all men to me!"

He sees the shallowness, the paltriness, the frailty of the heart; but he also sees its capacities, its possibilities, the mustard-seed germs of virtues and graces which the Spirit of God can unfold. We measure men too much by their powers, and not enough by their capacities, by what they are today and not by what they may become later on. It was because the eyes of Jesus swept the future that he could stand around the wreckage of a race in ruins and say, "Be of good cheer!"

Confidence in You

This indomitable Optimist has confidence in you. You have no hope for yourself. He has. You see your weakness, sordidness, vileness; he sees deeper, and seeing deeper, he has hope for you. He sees your capacity for God. He knows what you can do when you have come to your senses. He sees deeper also into God. You have no adequate conception of the patience or the mercy of the Infinite Father. He has. You do not know what Infinite Love can accomplish. He does. Because of your transgressions, you have lost faith in yourself. He has not. Because you have failed a thousand times, you say there is no use trying any more. He says, "Try again!" If you give yourself to him, he will make of you an optimist!

10

"Get thee behind me, Satan."

MATTHEW 16:23 KJV

THE FIRMNESS OF JESUS

Let us now think of the firmness of Jesus. Of his tenderness we think often, and also of his gentleness and graciousness. To these lovely graces the heart is joyfully responsive, and in dwelling upon them, we are likely to overlook other traits no less beautiful and praiseworthy. Gentleness of nature is not a virtue unless it is accompanied by tenacity of will. Sweetness of disposition is not enough to make a man useful and noble. Along with the sweetness there must go strength, and underneath the moods soft as velvet there must lie a resoluteness hard as steel.

The weakness of men under the play of social forces is one of the outstanding tragedies of history. To build a will strong enough to resist and control these forces is the central and crucial task of education. It is an ancient adage that evil companionships corrupt good morals. All men are more or less molded by the society of which they form a part. This impressionability is not a trait peculiar to childhood, but is carried with us through every stage of life. The young man in college is powerfully influenced by those of his classmates who are the nearest to him, and sometimes a few bold, masterful spirits will set the pace for a thousand men. Businessmen are as susceptible as college students and yield in crowds to the influence of a few dominating minds.

Against the Tide

The slavery of the social world has long been a theme for moralists and satirists. He is indeed a strong character who dares run counter to the traditions and fashions of the world in which he moves. Humanity goes in crowds and droves, and no bondage is too absurd or galling to be submitted to. The majority of mortals are not strong enough to be themselves: They become echoes of their neighbors, and walk in paths marked out by others. There is a spirit of the age which leaves its impress on every mind. Even the mightiest men cannot free themselves entirely from it. As Lowell says, "Every man is the prisoner of his date." We apologize for great men and women of history, saying, "Remember the times in which they lived!"

But when we come to Jesus of Nazareth, we are in the presence of a man whom nobody swerved or dominated, who is so free from the bias of his race and so clean of the spirit of his age that he seems to belong to all races and all ages. He is not the Son of David but the Son of Man—just genuinely, supremely human. He is not a citizen of the first century only, but the contemporary of each succeeding generation. Immersed in an ocean of mighty forces which beat upon him furiously through every hour of his career, he resisted them all successfully by the indomitable energy of a victorious will, living a life unique in its beauty and achieving a work unmarred by the limitations either of time or place.

That he was not insensible to the dominant forces of his time, he himself has told us in the story of the temptation. His countrymen had formed definite ideas of the Messiah. He was to be a wonder worker and the manifestations of his power were to be spectacular and overwhelming. He was to trample opposing forces under his feet and make Palestine the center of the world. This was the dream; this was the expectation. The best men expected this, as did also the worst men. It is a dangerous thing to baffle popular expectations.

Wherever he went he heard the people clamoring for a king, a king who should rise to supremacy over the wrecked empire of Caesar. The nation was ripe for revolution. A word from him would, like a spark, have kindled a mighty conflagration. Expectations had been built up by men anointed by Jehovah, and these expectations were glowing hot. To fall in with their ideals was a great temptation, one so terrific that he told his apostles all about it. He assured them that during this temptation he had been wrestling with the very prince of infernal powers, but that despite repeated assaults, he had come out of the conflict victorious. In choosing the road which led to supremacy by way of Gethsemane and Golgotha, he renounced the ideals of his countrymen and disappointed their dearest expectations. The nation then hurled itself with frantic force against him, but he did not budge. He was the Rock of Ages.

When we study his life with attentive eyes, we see it was one long resistance to the forces of his age. He was a patriot, but he could not go with his countrymen in any of their patriotic programs or expectations. He was a churchman, but he could not go with the members of the Jewish church in their favorite teachings and ceremonies. The religious teachers taught doctrines of the Sabbath which he could not accept. They presented forms of worship which he could not submit to. They laid down lines of separation which

> Gentleness of nature is not a virtue unless it is accompanied by tenacity of will.

it was impossible for him to observe. It is not easy to run counter to the deep-seated feelings of the most religious people of one's day, or to cut across the grain of the prejudices of the most conscientious men in the town. There were many reasons why Jesus should have conformed to the ideas and customs of the church, but he firmly resisted all the voices which urged him toward conformity, standing out alone in defiance of what the best men were doing and saying.

His nonconformity seemed to the majority to be impiety and to many blasphemy. For a godly man to be classed among blasphemers is one of the bitterest experiences which the heart can know. But Jesus paid the price and continued firm.

Firm with the Ruling Powers

Men of light and leading have an influence surpassing that of ordinary men. There were men in Palestine who, by learning and position, had won the confidence and esteem of their countrymen. As leaders and teachers of the people, they had their plans and systems, and into these they attempted to work this young man from Galilee. They recognized in him a man of force, and to manipulate him and make use of him was a natural ambition. No man with a noble cause to promote will lightly antagonize the most influential men of his day. He will bend to them so far as he is able; he will yield to their whims and caprices so far as conscience will permit; he will go with them so far as this is possible; but, if he is a man of strength, he will not compromise his principles, and he will never jeopardize the victory of his cause by playing into the hands of men whose faces are toward a different goal.

Jesus could not be manipulated. He refused to be used. One party after another tried to work him into its scheme, but he was incorrigibly intractable and went on his way independent, unshackled, free. All the seductions offered by the men who sat on thrones could not swerve him from his course, and although his steadfastness made him enemies and finally nailed him to the cross, he was everywhere and always a man who could not be moved.

Firm with His Friends

There are men who are too strong to be manipulated by their foes, but in the hands of their friends, they are plastic as wax. Jesus could not be manipulated even by his friends. He had many friends in

Galilee, but he never gave up his principles to please them. They had their prejudices and superstitions, but he never surrendered to them. He knew their bigotry and narrowness, and so, in his opening sermon, he read the story of God's compassion on a Syrian leper and also on a Sidonian widow. His sermon raised the storm which he had anticipated, but he bore the fury of it without flinching. He would not keep silence when he knew he ought to speak, nor would he turn aside from the path he knew he ought to travel—even though, by sticking to the path, he made himself a lifelong exile.

But probably no friend in Galilee was ever so near to Jesus' heart as Simon Peter. At a crises in Jesus' life Peter did his best to dissuade Jesus from a certain course, but the loyal and loving friend succeeded no better than the most hostile Pharisee. This man of Nazareth could not be moved by friend or foe. It was his Father's business he was attending to, and therefore all efforts to draw him aside were made in vain. "Get thee behind me, Satan" [Mark 8:33 KJV], he said to the astonished Peter, recognizing in him the same evil spirit he had

> Immersed in an ocean of mighty forces which beat upon him furiously through every hour of his career, he resisted them all successfully.

contended with years before in the desert. To defy the threats of powerful enemies is hard, but to turn a deaf ear to the dissuasions of loving friends is harder still. Only a man of unconquerable will is equal to a test so taxing. Jesus met it and did not fail.

It was a test he faced in his own home, also. His brothers did not understand him. From their standpoint he often did the injudicious thing and refused to do the thing which would have forwarded his reputation. They were always ready with advice. He could not take it. They urged him to go to Jerusalem at a time when he could not go. They exhorted him to go home at a time when his duty was to be somewhere else. Only a man who has been driven by conscience to go contrary to the wishes of members of his own family can enter into the experience which Jesus suffered or can measure the strength of will which one must have to resist successfully the importunities of love.

This test of willpower reached its climax in Jesus' conflict with his mother. She loved him and he loved her, but he could not always carry out her wishes. There comes a time in many a man's life when even his own mother's exhortations must go unheeded in order to obey a higher call. Such an experience came to Jesus. It was a sword through Mary's heart, and it was a sword also through the heart of Jesus. That painful experience in the Temple at the age of twelve was probably not the first of its kind in Jesus' life, and it was certainly not the last. The ties to Mary were not so deep as the ties which bound Jesus to the heavenly Father, and when Mary's wish conflicted with the Father's will, the wish of the woman was put aside to make room for the will of God.

Here, then, we have a situation which is distressing indeed. The most tender and gracious and obliging of men is compelled to resist not only the prayers of his countrymen but the wishes of his family and friends. He stands like a rock in the midst of a troubled sea, and all its billows dash themselves against his feet in vain. There was something inflexible in his will, something granitic in his soul. When he found a man whom he thought worthy to be one of his first disciples, he called him "rock." It is certain that Jesus loved stability in others, and what he loved in others, he had superabundantly in himself. Firm himself, he loved men who could not be moved. Unconquerable himself, he entrusted his Gospel to men who would endure. Men who put their hand to the plow but looked back were not men he could make use of in the saving of a world.

Unchanging Firmness

It is in this tenacity of will that we find an indispensable element of Christian character. Men are to resist exterior forces and form their life from within. They are not to be swayed by current opinion, but by the Spirit of the Eternal in their heart. They are not to listen to the voices of time, but to live and work for eternity. We like this steadfastness in human character, and we also crave it in God. Men have always loved to think of Him as the unchanging and the unchangeable, the one "with whom can be no variation, neither shadow that is cast by turning." ["with whom is no variableness, neither shadow of turning" James 1:17 KJV.] And what we desire in God, we find in Jesus of Nazareth. He also is unchanging and unchangeable. A writer of the first century encourages the hearts of his readers by reminding them that "Jesus Christ is the same yesterday and today, yes and forever" [Hebrews 13:8 NASB]. Jesus never called himself the Rock, but the Christian heart soon gave him that appellation, and few hymns have proved so popular in the English-speaking world as

> *Rock of Ages, cleft for me!*
> *Let me hide myself in thee.*

What Jesus was in Palestine, he is today and shall be for evermore. All his promises stand unshaken; all his warnings remain unchanged. His attitude to sinners is today what it has been from the beginning and what it will be to the end. You cannot discourage him by your ingratitude; you cannot make him other than he is by your disobedience. He is not broken down by human folly or driven from his plan by human perversity. From age to age he is about his Father's business, and in the midst of all nations and kindreds and tongues, he goes about doing good.

11

"It is more blessed to give
than to receive."
ACTS 20:35 KJV

THE GENEROSITY OF JESUS

In the above passage Paul is speaking farewell words to the officers of the church to which he has given more time and love than to any other. He reminds them of things he has often said to them before, and in closing calls to their minds one of the most illuminating and helpful of all the sayings of the Master: "It is more blessed to give than to receive." These words express with rare fullness one of the finest of the traits of Jesus: his generosity.

If one were asked to mention a half dozen key-words of Christian duty, he would be sure to place the word "give" high in the list. One cannot read the New Testament without being halted by that word, for it occurs repeatedly and always with an emphasis which arrests the heart. Indeed, it has been often claimed that the Man of Galilee is wild and reckless in his theory of giving. His saying, "Give to the one who asks you, and do not turn away from the one who wants to borrow from you" [Matthew 5:42 NIV], has been to many a mystery and an offense. But the exhortation need stagger no one if it is remembered that all action is to be subjected to the limitations of love. Mortals are urged to give as God gives, and God's giving is always fashioned and conditioned by his love. He does not give to every

115

man the precise thing which the man asks for. He says to all of us not once, but many times, "No," "no," "no!"

Giving Generously

Love can never give where giving would work hurt. The mother cannot give the razor to the little girl who pleads for it, nor can the father grant his son every favor which he asks. The man half drunk who begs for a quarter on the street corner must be refused, and in every case the petitioner must be dealt with according to the requirements of the law of love. But to write down all the considerations and qualifications which must be taken into account in dealing with a world which is always asking was, for Jesus, a plain impossibility. Jesus threw out the great word "give," unqualified and naked, allowing it to speak unhindered to the human heart, as a word which holds in it a revelation of the mind of God. Luke tells us that one day when Jesus was unfolding his idea of generosity, he said: "Give, and it will be given to you. A good measure, pressed down, shaken together and running over, will be poured into your lap. For with the measure you use, it will be measured to you" [Luke 6:38 NIV]. To understand this you must have been some time on a farm and watched the farmer measure grains or small fruits. The pressing down and the shaking together and the running over all are graphic and meaningful expressions intended to picture to the mind the kind of measure in which the king of heaven takes delight.

A man who does not skimp or dole out with a stingy hand is, says Jesus, a man whom the universe likes and blesses. He will lose nothing by his liberality, for the world is constructed on a generous principle; and by surrendering himself to the divine spirit of giving, he will be in tune with the Infinite, and shall, by no means, lose his reward. He need not be anxious about the precise time when such action shall bring its recompense. It is enough to go forward, giving and asking nothing in return, assured that somewhere and somehow his recompense shall be forthcoming. Let him, therefore, when he makes a dinner or supper, not invite simply his friends or his brethren, or his kindred or his rich neighbors, expecting that they will invite him again. Let him feast the poor, the maimed, the lame, the blind, men who cannot give anything in return, and then let him expect from God the blessing which is provided for the generous heart. That blessing may not come in all its fullness in the world that now is, but there will be a complete recompense at the resurrection of the just. What Jesus said to his disciples he says to all, "Freely you have received, freely give" [Matthew 10:8 NIV].

Blessings and Curses

Jesus' dislike of the close–fisted and parsimonious heart comes out in several of his parables. For example, when he speaks of Dives in his fine linen at his banquet-table while the sick beggar eats crumbs at his gate, we can feel the hot flame of an indignant soul. And where in the New Testament will you find more exuberant praise than that which he lavishes upon the woman who poured a year's salary's worth of perfume on his head and feet? Miserly souls near him were offended by such extravagance, but he liked it. He appreciated the lavish expenditures of love. When he sees a poor widow throwing her two bits of copper into the treasury in the temple, all the money she had in the world, he does not criticize her for doing a foolish thing as most of us would have done, but he cries out in a shout which has in it the music of a hallelujah, "This poor widow has put in more than all the others" [Luke 21:3 NIV]. In a world so filled with grudging and close-fisted men, it cheered his great heart to see now and then a person who had mastered the divine art of giving.

Ultimate Generosity

When he said that it is more blessed to give than to receive, he was speaking from personal experience. He had not read that in a book. He had found it out in life. When he urged men to give freely, abundantly, lavishly, gladly, continually, he was only preaching what he himself practiced. He had no money to give, but he gave without stint what he had. He had time and he gave it. The golden hours were his, and he gave them. He gave them all. So recklessly did he give them that, in order to find time to pray, it was necessary to use hours when other men were sleeping. He had strength, and he gave it with a liberality which astonished and alarmed his friends.

> This, then, was the earthly career of Jesus— one continuous manifestation of generous and boundless love.

He poured out his energy to the last ounce. At one time we see him seated, exhausted, on the curbing of Jacob's well; at another time we see him falling asleep as soon as his head touched the pillow on the little boat which was carrying him back to Capernaum. When, on the last day of his life, they laid a beam of timber upon his shoulder, he staggered under it and then fell, so completely had he been exhausted by the arduous labors of the preceding months and years. He saved others, but himself he did not know how to save. He had thought, and he gave it. He had ideas, and he scattered them. He had truth, and he shared it with men.

Behold a sower goes forth to sow! It is Jesus. Look at him. Watch the swing of that arm. What a generous arm! He scatters the seed upon the beaten path. No matter. He scatters the seed on the soil that is rocky. What of it? He scatters the seed in brier patches and thorny corners. He does not mind that. The seed is abundant, and he will scatter it with a lavish hand, hoping that some of it will find the soil which is fertile and which will bring forth a harvest to make glad the heart of God. Many a teacher has saved his best ideas for a chosen few; Jesus scattered his. He had often ignorant and prejudiced and unresponsive hearers, but he threw his pearls by the handful wherever he went. What glorious ideas he scattered over the crowds of Galilean farmers! What heavenly truths he unfolded to men and women of whom the world took no notice!

Never was a teacher such a spendthrift in the squandering of ideas; never did a great thinker pour out his treasures in such wild and immeasurable profusion. Freely he had received, and therefore freely he gave. It was not merely the work of the intellect, but also the blood of the heart which he gave. His affection toward men flowed in a stream constant and full. His sympathy covered all classes, and no individual, however low and despised, ever appealed to him in vain. Blind men, on hearing of his approach, lined themselves along the road crying as he passed, "Have mercy also on us." Lepers who were counted unclean and treated worse than dogs ventured to push their way into his presence and ask for a healing touch. Samaritans, the very offscourings of the world, in the estimation of the orthodox Jew, knew that in this new rabbi they had a benefactor and friend. When he drove the traders out of the Temple, it was the blind and the lame who came to him, knowing that they would not be cast away.

Love Gives All

Sympathy eats up the blood of the veins, and he who sympathizes draws heavily on the fountains of energy. This Jesus always did. He was a man with a loving heart. He loved both his friends and his enemies. He loved them at the beginning, and he loved them to the end. The love which he lavished upon his disciples purified them and bound them to him with bonds which nothing could break. But his love went out also to those who hated him and screamed to bring about his death. "Father, forgive them, for they know not what they do" [Luke 23:34 KJV]: It is in such a prayer that the loving heart of Jesus is clearly revealed. He poured out his love with a generosity which reminded men of the generosity of God.

Having given time and strength and thought and sympathy and love, he finally gave up his life. More than this can no man give. He was not an unwilling victim of circumstances, or the helpless prey of ungovernable political forces, or an assassination victim like Caesar or Lincoln. He gave his life consciously and deliberately. It was not snatched from him by accident or fate, but freely surrendered by a heart willing to pay the great price. Again and again he endeavored to make this plain. "I have power to lay down my life," he said, "and I have power to take it again." It was his conviction from the beginning that he came into the world to minister to men's needs, and to give his life as a ransom for many. It was only by the giving of his life that he could soften men's hearts and bring a lost world back to the Father's house.

Lessons from Nature

This, then, was the earthly career of Jesus—one continuous manifestation of generous and boundless love. In his character we see not only what is possible for man to be, but we also behold a revelation of the character of the Eternal. "Anyone who has seen me has seen the Father" [John 14:9 NIV], so said Jesus to those who were the nearest to him, and it is a saying which should be often in our thoughts. In studying the character of Jesus, we get light not only upon the possibilities of man, but also upon the disposition and the will of God.

The God revealed by Jesus is the same God revealed by Nature. The God of Nature has always been known as a generous God. The days and nights, the sky and sea and land, the changing seasons, all bear witness to His amazing generosity. He is extravagant in all His doings. He is lavish in all His benefactions. He scatters good things with the bountiful munificence of a King. He scatters the stars not in paltry thousands, but in countless millions. He creates flowers not in numbers which we can count, but in a profusion which confuses and confounds the imagination. He always gives more than can be accepted. He throws sunsets away on eyes which do not care for them. He gives fruit trees more blossoms than the trees can use. At every feast which He spreads, there are fragments remaining filling twelve baskets. He is a munificent, free-handed, bountiful and extravagant God!

In the realm of nature He is assuredly a lavish and bewilderingly bounteous God, and what He is in the world of nature, He is likewise in the realm of the spirit. Jesus says, "Ask and you will receive" [John 16:24 NIV]. Do not hesitate to do it. No matter who you are, you may do it. "For everyone who asks receives" [Luke 11:10 NIV]. It is an eternal principle, deep-seated in creation and deep-rooted in the heart of God, that gifts rich and royal may be had for the asking. It is the purpose of the Christian religion to bring us to a God who is willing to give us above what we are willing to ask or able to think. Jesus' message thrills with the thought that we constantly get, not what we earn or what we deserve, but what an ungrudging and open-handed God is delighted to give.

Love Never Counts

If you ask why Jesus was generous, the answer is that God is love. When was love anything but liberal? When has love ever dealt out good things with a scant and skimping and miserly hand? When Peter suggested a certain number as being enough to indicate the limits of forgiveness, Jesus told him not to count at all. Love never counts. When did a mother ever count the number of times she kissed her baby? And when did a friend ever catalogue the number of favors toward his friend? Or when did a parent ever make a list of all the good things he gave his children? Love never counts. It is the nature of love to give, and to keep on giving, and then to devise new ways of larger giving, and to imagine still additional needs which may be supplied.

Speaking to fathers, Jesus says: "Which of you, if his son asks for bread, will give him a stone? Or if he asks for a fish, will give him a snake? If you then, though you are evil, know how to give good gifts to your children, how much more will your Father in heaven give good gifts to those who ask him!" [Matthew 7:9-11 NIV]. If you are ever tempted to question the generosity of the heart of God, look at Jesus! Once in the world's history there has lived a man whose supreme joy was ungrudging giving. He knew as no other man has ever known how much more blessed it is to give than to receive. He lived not to be ministered unto, but to minister; not to receive, but to give; not to save his life, but to pour it out for others. If generosity so great has appeared in Time, it must be because there is a generous heart in Eternity; if a grace so beautiful has blossomed on our earth, we have a right to expect the same grace in heaven.

> "I came to cast fire upon the earth."
>
> LUKE 12:49 NASB

THE ENTHUSIASM OF JESUS

Strange to say, the word "enthusiasm" does not occur in our English New Testament, nor is it to be found in the Greek Testament. Yet, the New Testament is the most enthusiastic of all books, and Jesus is the most enthusiastic of all men. The word "enthusiasm" is avoided and for a reason. In the first century it had unsavory associations. Enthusiasm in the Pagan world was "an ecstasy, or divine possession." An enthusiast was "one who was inspired or possessed by a god." Often the enthusiast was a fanatic; sometimes he was a madman. The evangelists and apostles did not like the word, and so they kept it out of their writings. In the speech of today, enthusiasm is a noble word. It is fervor of mind, ardency of spirit, exaltation of soul. It is passion, heat, fire, zeal. Though the word is absent, the thing itself is present. Jesus burns with fervent heat. His very words are sparks which kindle conflagrations.

A Man Driven

When a boy, he visited Jerusalem with his parents, and slipping one day into the Temple to hear the scholars discussing the great problems of religion, he lost himself. He forgot what day of the week it was and what hour of the day it was. His father and mother and brothers and sisters and friends all passed completely from his mind. He plunged headlong into the discussion of the doctors, gave himself up completely to the subject of the hour, allowed himself to be swept along on the tide of thought and discussion, until all at once his mother's face appeared at the door, and he was reminded of the place he had left vacant in the caravan which had started toward Galilee. In this Temple experience we see a nature sensitive and impressionable, capable of being heated to high temperatures.

When, as a young man of thirty, he next appears before us, we see him at the river Jordan being baptized by the mighty preacher John. Immediately after the baptism, Mark tells us he was "driven" [KJV] by the Spirit into the wilderness. The word "driven" has in it a significance which is revealing. Jesus is so full of feeling after the experience which came to him in his baptism that he cannot linger near the homes of men, but must at once rush away into unfrequented and desert places where he can meditate upon the strange thing that has happened to him and ponder the steps which he must next take.

From this time on we have a man before us who is being driven. Even when a boy he used a word which expressed the intensity of his feeling, "Do you not know that I must be about my Father's business?" He never ceased to use that word: "must." They wanted him to stay in Capernaum, but he could not do it. "I must preach the gospel of the kingdom of God to the other cities also." They wanted him to stay away from Jerusalem, knowing that it was dangerous there, but he said, "I must go to Jerusalem. I have a baptism to undergo, and how distressed I am until it is completed!" He felt that his life would be short, and so he kept saying, "I must work the works of Him that sent me while it is day: the night cometh when no man can work" [John 9:4 KJV].

'Out of the Overflow'

How intense his life was we can see in what is told us of his habit of praying. He was always praying. He arose early in the morning in order to find more time to pray; he stayed up late at night in order to increase the hours in which he might speak to God. Sometimes he did not go to bed at all, remaining all night long upon some hilltop under the stars pouring out his soul to God. He was enthusiastic in prayer, and therefore he was zealous in work. Men were astounded by the magnitude of his labors. Sometimes he did not take time to eat. Even when he went away for a season of relaxation, he gave himself up to the crowds which pursued him.

His words have in them an energy which burns. Again and again we catch expressions in which we can feel his great heart beating: "I have not found so great faith, no, not in Israel" [Luke 7:9 KJV]; "Woman, you have great faith!" [Matthew 15:28 NIV]; "I praise you, Father!" [Luke 10:21 NIV]; "O Jerusalem, Jerusalem...how often..." [Luke 13:34 KJV]. All these are out of the throat of an enthusiast, a man surcharged with feeling. At the distance of nineteen hundred years from the day on which they were spoken, our hearts leap when we listen to them. The rains of the centuries have not put out their fire!

But it is not simply what Jesus says, but also what those who touched him say, which lets us look into the molten center of his glowing heart. Mark frankly tells us that there was a time in Jesus' life when his labor was so excessive that his friends said, "He is beside himself" [Mark 3:21 KJV]. Expressive, indeed, is the phrase. A man is beside himself when he is a little "off." When a man has swung just a little from his balance, he is beside himself. He is in the borderland which is between sanity and insanity.

Zeal Works

Such burning earnestness in the work of doing good had never been seen in Palestine. No wonder men said, "He is beside himself!"

But this was the judgment of his friends. His enemies did not hesitate to say boldly, "He has a devil; he is mad." Jesus made this impression not once, but often. Such zeal for righteousness, such enthusiasm for helping men, seemed to the cold-blooded scribes the fury of a maniac. It was when Paul was burning with the same kind of heat that Festus cried, "Paul, you're out of your mind" [Acts 12:15 NIV]. Nothing seems so crazy as enthusiasm to a man incapable of feeling it.

The crowds also bear witness to the fire which this man had in him. He stirred men up wherever he went. Again and again the excitement rose to fever heat, and Jesus slipped away and hid himself. Near the close of his career the crowds went wild in their tumultuous joy, shouting, singing, casting their clothing in the dust that the animal which Jesus rode might have a carpet for its hoofs like unto that furnished for triumphal processions of kings. No man can set a crowd blazing unless his own soul is ablaze. When we see some men hurrahing and adoring and other men gnashing their teeth and cursing, it is evident we are in the presence of a man whose heart glows like a furnace and whose soul radiates heat wherever he goes.

The Twelve

A still finer evidence of this is found in the character of the men whom Jesus attracted to him as his intimate friends. The apostles were all men of fire. Do not believe the pictures when they paint the twelve as limp and pallid men. They were full-blooded, virile, mighty men, full of fire and passion, drawn to Jesus because in him they saw a man who fulfilled them.

Peter had a seething soul; his words roll out of him like molten lava. John and James were called Sons of Thunder. The disciple whom Jesus loved was so passionate that he wanted to burn up a whole town which had insulted his Master. One of the disciples was a zealot, a member of the most radical political party in Palestine. Men of this party could scarcely sleep, so intense was their hatred of Rome, and no man among the zealots could ever have been attracted by a cold-blooded, limp-handed man.

It was because Jesus had in him the fire which the zealots loved that Simon enrolled himself among the apostles. If there was a lethargic temperament in the apostolic company, it was that of Thomas; but even he was so devoted to Jesus that he said to his comrades, "Come, let us go and die with him." That was the feeling of them all. They loved Jesus with such an intensity of devotion, such a passionate self-abandon, that they were ready at any moment to lay down their lives for him. No man can win and hold the ardent devotion of strong men unless he has a soul which is hot. Jesus from first to last was surrounded by enthusiasts because he himself was enthusiastic.

Zeal's Roots

If you ask for the cause of this enthusiasm, you will find that it has three roots. In the first place, Jesus had a sensitive nature. He was finely organized; his nerves were delicately strung. There is a vast difference in the make-up of men. Some men are coarse, stolid, heavy. They have sensations but not intense ones. They have the emotions of vegetables. There are other men who are as delicately adjusted as an aeolian harp. Every breeze that blows over them causes them to vibrate and woos from them music. Such a man was Jesus. No finer clay was ever organized around a soul than that which formed his body, and this body was never coarsened or callused by sin. On the Mount of Transfiguration his soul so shone through his body that his disciples were awed and overwhelmed. In the Garden of Gethsemane his agony was so great that the perspiration on his brow was as drops of blood. When his soul at one time came into his face men fell backward to the ground.

Along with this nature capable of burning, there existed a vision of God and a vision of man which set the nation on fire. Jesus saw that the Maker of the universe is a Father; that at the center of things there beats a Father's heart; that over all there extends a Father's care; and that to all there flows a Father's love. Other men have seen this dimly, as it were through a glass darkly, but Jesus saw it as it had never been seen before and as it has never been seen since. It was to him the one clear and luminous fact of the universe, and everything else was seen in the glory of this stupendous truth. Since God is the all-Father, then all men are His children. He created them all. He loves them all. He desires to save them all. No matter who they are or what they are or where they are, they are His children, and they cannot drift beyond His love and care. Therefore, men everywhere are brothers, and for one brother to help another, this is the supreme joy in living. Other men see this dimly, but to Jesus it was all clear as the sun at noon.

> Out of such a nature, heated hot by such a vision, there came forth a purpose, steadfast and full of passion.

With such a vision of God and such a vision of man, is it to be wondered at that his soul burned like a star? Out of such a nature, heated hot by such a vision, there came forth a purpose, steadfast and full of passion. To the clear eye of Jesus a mighty battle was raging on the earth. There was a terrific conflict between right and wrong, light and darkness, good and evil, God and the Devil. There was nothing to do at such a crisis but to throw himself wholeheartedly into the contest, fighting indomitably for the glory of the Father and the welfare of his brethren. Put these three things together—a sensitive and flammable nature, a clear and glorious vision, and a fiery and indomitable purpose—and you have the ingredients which go to produce the divine flame which is known as enthusiasm.

Zeal's Drawing Power

What a beautiful thing is enthusiasm! Moses turned aside to see a burning bush, and everybody turns aside to see a burning man. Glance across the centuries, and you will note that every time the race has turned aside from the beaten path, it has been to see a man who was burning. Enthusiasm is of different kinds, but every kind is fascinating. But higher than all enthusiasms is the fire that burns in souls in love with God. To know Him, to serve Him, to glorify Him, this is the highest ambition of which the soul is capable, and the soul, when possessed with this ambition, burns with a fire that cannot be quenched. This was the enthusiasm of Jesus. In him the highest of the enthusiasms reached its climax. He lived and moved and had his being in the presence of the Eternal. From the beginning to the end he saw the majesty of righteousness, loved the beauty of holiness, and lived for the glory of God.

Zeal's Fire

It is not to be wondered at, then, that the religion of Jesus likes the word "fire." John the Baptist declared that he could baptize only with water but that one was coming who would baptize with fire. From John's hands men came dripping; from Jesus' hands they came blazing. Luke tells us that on the Day of Pentecost there were flames above every head—not surprising. John, on the isle of Patmos thinking of Jesus, sees him with eyes like flames of fire and feet of burnished brass. He hears him talking to the Laodiceans, and this is what he says, "I know your deeds, that you are neither cold nor hot. I wish you were either one or the other! So, because you are lukewarm...I am about to spit you out of my mouth " [Revelation 3:15-16 NIV]. One can drink cold water with a relish. He can also drink water heated to a certain temperature. But against tepid water the stomach rebels. The beloved disciple does not hesitate to represent Jesus saying, "Lukewarm Christians are nauseating to me!"

What is the matter with Christians that they are so lacking in enthusiasm? The answer is that the nature is saturated, soaked by the chilling drizzle of worldliness, and along with this deterioration of nature comes a diminishing of the vision of the Fatherhood of God and the Brotherhood of man. Because of this shadowed vision, the glowing purpose is also lacking, and the soul does not catch fire. What, then, shall we do? Let us go back to Him who is a zealous God, so eager and ardent in His love that He gave His only begotten Son. If we are not ablaze in the presence of such a Gospel, it is because we have a heart of stone; but He who knows our frame and who remembers that we are dust has promised to remove the heart of stone and give us a heart of flesh.

"Rejoice, and be exceeding glad."
MATTHEW 5:12 KJV

THE GLADNESS OF JESUS

Pushing all the poets and philosophers aside, let us ask ourselves the question: Did Jesus of Nazareth impress men as glad or sad, solemn or radiant, jubilant or melancholy? There is no doubt about the answer which the painters give. They nearly always paint him sad; they love to paint him on the cross; they picture him dying with a great melancholy in his eyes—or if they do not paint him on the cross, they paint him on the way to the cross with the crown of thorns on his head, bending under the burden as he staggers up Golgotha. The Jesus of Christian history is a man of sorrows and acquainted with grief; there is sadness in his face and a great pang in his heart. And not only do the painters paint him sad, but so also does our imagination. When we think of him, we think of him as crucified. We always see him with the shadow of the cross upon him; we always think of him as severe and sad. But we cannot afford to follow the painters. They paint Jesus with a halo. Nobody in Jerusalem ever saw the halo. They paint him with a shadow on his face—do you supposed the men in Palestine saw the shadow? We want to see him as he was.

Enemies' Evidence

In order to find out what impression he really made upon the people of his day, it will be worth our while to listen to what his enemies had to say. Of course his enemies will not speak the ungarbled truth—they will deal in falsehoods—but even falsehoods are of great advantage in trying to make one's way toward the truth. There is nothing that so dumfounds a lawyer in the questioning of a witness as unbroken silence. If a witness will only speak, if he will only speak falsehoods, his speech is more illuminating than continuous silence; for falsehoods, when arranged in a row, have a curious fashion of pointing in the direction of the truth. When a man begins lying, if you can only keep him lying long enough, he will eventually put you on the track of discovering what the truth is.

So it is with the enemies of Jesus. They have said certain things which are invaluable to us in our search after authentic knowledge of the character of Jesus. Among other things which they said, they declared he was a glutton. Of course he was not, but they said he was. Now a glutton is never a glum and sour-faced man. Gluttony is a form of pleasure; men overeat because overeating gives enjoyment. A glutton is likely to be round and rotund. When the men of Jesus' day said he was a glutton, we may rest assured he was not an ascetic in his looks or habits.

They also called him a wine bibber. Of course he was not, but the very fact that they accursed him of guzzling wine points in the direction of the kind of man he was. A wine bibber is usually a jolly man. Wine unlocks the lips and gives temporary brilliancy to the mind. A man under the influence of wine is exceedingly social and talkative and genial. The enemies of Jesus would never have called him a wine bibber if he had been as glum and sad as some of the artists have painted him!

They called him also the friend of Publicans and sinners. By "Publicans and sinners" we are to understand nonchurchgoers. This man not only went to church and associated with pious people, but he associated with people who had no piety at all. When they declared he was a friend of these nonchurchgoers, they implied that he was of the same stripe as they: "Birds of a feather always flock together." He would never have associated with such godless people if he himself had not had a godless heart, or so his enemies declared. And if Jesus had been taciturn and sullen, grim and morose, his enemies would never have declared he was a companion of light-hearted men. Their lying would have taken another form. Put, then, these three bits of falsehood together, and what is the direction in which they point? They are the most precious bits of slander that ever slipped from slimy lips. They prove indisputably that whatever Jesus was or was not, he was not morose or sour or melancholy.

Jesus As a Key Witness

Having listened to the testimony of his enemies, let us now study one of the words Jesus applied to himself. There were pious people in Palestine who were greatly scandalized because Jesus never fasted, nor did he teach his disciples that it was their duty to fast. Fasting was a recognized feature of the Jewish religion. Every person of orthodox piety in Palestine fasted twice every week. Fasting had been prescribed by the greatest of the rabbis; it had also been the requirement of John the Baptist himself. Some people came to Jesus one day in disgust, saying, "Why do your disciples not fast?" The reply of Jesus is illuminating. He said, "How can the children of the bride chamber fast when the bridegroom is with them?" Did you ever mark the use of the word "bridegroom"? Jesus says that he is a bridegroom. He seized upon a word that is the symbol of human joy. If ever a man is happy in this world, it is on his wedding day. Jesus says that he lives in an atmosphere of wedding joy and so also do his disciples. It is impossible, therefore, for either him or his disciples to take up any of the old fashions of the grim and solemn piety of the past.

He told the men who criticized him that his life was different from the life of John the Baptist, and also from the life of the Pharisees. You cannot mix the two kinds of piety; the two forms of life will not mingle. Let me give you an illustration or two, he said: "A man does not put a new patch on an old garment, because the new patch will tear out and the rent will be still worse. Neither can you put my form of life onto the old form of piety. The two will not hold together; the strength that is in my form of life will simply tear the old form of life to pieces. Or, to give you another illustration, men do not put new wine into old wine skins, for there is too much life and movement and sparkle in a new wine for the old skins. If you attempt to put the new wine into the old skins, the old skins will burst and the wine will be lost. So do not think that you can put the new life which I live and which I want all rny followers to live into old forms of pharisaic piety, for this cannot be done. I am living a new kind of life, and I want a new kind of man, a new spirit, a new form of religion."

Joy Lessons

It would seem, then, that Jesus was a man abounding in joy. Gladness was one of the notes of his character. Listen to him as he teaches, and again and again you catch the notes of happiness. He was all the time saying, "Unless you become like a little child, you cannot enter the kingdom of God"—and what was it in the little child that attracted him? One thing which attracted him was the child's sunny heart. What would we do in this world without the children laughing away the cares and sighs? Have you ever listened to their laughter in the streets while the funeral procession was passing by? Have you ever seen a little child with beaming face at the center of a room in which there was a casket around which broken-hearted men and women were gathering? Look at that child in the center of the chamber of death—that is the picture of the Christian amid the shadows of this darkened world.

Or listen again to what Jesus says about worry. He defines it as one of the deadliest of all sins. We are not to worry about the present, about the necessities of existence, about tomorrow, about what we ought to do or say in the great crises which lie ahead of us. It is not right, he says; it is contrary to the law of God. Look at nature: See the lilies and the birds— there is not a trace of solicitude in all nature's lovely face. Listen

> Jesus says that he is a bridegroom. He seized upon a word that is the symbol of human joy.

again to the exhortations which he gives his disciples. He tells them that when men persecute them and say all manner of evil against them falsely, they are to rejoice and be exceeding glad. The English translation does not do justice to the Greek. He says, "Rejoice and leap for joy," or in other words, let your joy express itself. When matters are at their worst, then you ought to have the happiness which leaps. Certainly a sad-hearted man could never give advice like that.

Listen to him again as he says to the great crowds, "Come to me all you who are weary and burdened, and I will give you rest...for my yoke is easy and my burden is light" [Matthew 11:28, 30 NIV]. A glum-faced prophet could never speak so. He was glad even to the end. Even in the upper chamber, with death only a few hours away, he goes right on speaking of the joy that is bubbling up in his own heart, and he prays that the same joy may abound in the hearts of those who love him. He tells his disciples that all of his teaching has been granted unto them because of his desire that his joy might remain in them and that their joy might be full. There was no shadow on his face that night in the upper chamber. The cross is near, but it casts no shadow.

Jesus Laughed!

But does not the New Testament say that Jesus wept? It does. And does the New Testament ever say that Jesus laughed? It does not. Are we therefore to infer that Jesus often wept and never laughed? The inference is unfounded. Why does the New Testament say that Jesus wept? Probably because it was so exceptional. It is the exceptional thing that is written down. For example thousands of people walk the New York City streets, but let one of them fall and break his leg and that accident is noted. No attention is paid to the thousands who meet with no accident.

Jesus laughed so frequently it was not worthwhile calling attention to it. He wept so seldom that when he did weep, it struck the disciples with consternation. John could never forget it. He remembered the day at the tomb of Lazarus when Mary was weeping and her sister and all the relatives and friends, and it was then that Jesus wept, so tender and sympathetic was he that he broke down—that great strong, radiant, exuberant man wept. John says that the world itself could not contain the books that could be written if he attempted to put down all the things which Jesus said and did. He will crowd back a million things to make room for that one surprising fact that at the grave of Lazarus: Jesus wept. The sentence, instead of proving that Jesus was lachrymose and doleful, bears eloquent witness to the fact that Jesus was buoyant and exultant.

A Christian must then, if he would follow Jesus, be a joyous and jubilant man. You may be tempted to say that glum and dismal Christians are not Christians at all. That is probably somewhat too severe. It would be nearer right to say that they are not developed Christians, mature or ripened Christians. The very finest apples, you know, in the earlier stages of their growth are sour and green. It is not until the sun has done his perfect work that they are golden and luscious. Just so it is with souls in the earlier stages of development—they are often green and sour, crabbed, and full of acid. But if they will only subject themselves to the shining of the sun, the great joyous, exuberant, laughing sun, all the juices of their nature will grow sweet and mellow, and they will find themselves at last in the kingdom of peace and joy.

It is the tragedy of this world that there are so many people in it who find it impossible to rejoice. What is the matter with you that you are not happier than you are? Certainly there is something wrong! What a pity it is to live in a world like this and not enjoy living! It is amazing that anyone should live in a universe so glorious and not feel like shouting! If you are lachrymose and drooping, it is because there is something wrong. You are not well in body or in mind, or it may be you are sick in both. You have not yet learned the high art of living; you have not yet come to Jesus. Why not come and sit at his feet? Why not take his yoke upon you and learn of him, for his yoke is easy and his burden is light.

"I am meek and lowly in heart."
MATTHEW 11:29 KJV

THE HUMILITY OF JESUS

Let us begin with that wonderful verse in Matthew 11: "Come unto me, all ye that labor and are heavy laden; and I will give you rest. Take my yoke upon you, and learn of me; for I am meek and lowly in heart: and ye shall find rest unto your souls" (vv. 28-30 KJV). That sentence is unique in the Gospel. There is nothing else at all like it. It is a bit of autobiography which is immeasurably precious. Nowhere is Jesus recorded as having said, "Come unto me, for I am patient—for I am courageous—for I am self-sacrificing"; but here, for the first time, he calls attention to one of his characteristics. He has allowed other men to call attention to this virtue or that grace, but he himself will bring out the fact that he is humble. At this point he takes the brush in his own hand, saying, "I will put this color on myself."

So unusual is the sentence that some men have been scandalized by it. They have declared he never said it, that it is not like him, that he could not say it, that if he did say it, it reveals a defect in his character. These men tell us that a man cannot eulogize himself, that it is always improper for a man to sing his own praises. All of which may be true, but this is a fair question: Is it right for a man ever to describe himself? Is it proper for a man to give a reason why men should come to him and take lessons of him? I think it is. That is all

Jesus does in this instance. He says, "Come unto me. I have some-thing to teach you; I should like to teach you humility."

The World's Definition vs. God's

Possibly no other virtue in the catalog of Christian virtues is so misunderstood as this one. No other one has been so often errone-ously defined; no other grace has been so persistently counterfeited and caricatured. What do we mean by humility? If you should have asked that question in the streets of ancient Athens, men would have told you that humility is something mean; it is cowardly, cringing, grov-eling; humility is meanness of spirit; it is something low and selfish; it is a characteristic of slaves. If a Greek had called another Greek humble, the Greek would have been in-sulted by the epithet. In all the Pagan world there was no virtue known as humility. Humility was always and everywhere a defect, a blemish, a vice.

> Certainly humility on the lips of Jesus does not mean a low estimate of one's powers.

But what do we mean by humility? The question is not so easily answered as it might seem. Humility is a Christian virtue—everybody says it is. We know that Jesus was humble. We know also that he demands humility of us. We know that he took the ancient word and cleansed it and made it a lovely word, and yet when asked to define the meaning of it, how difficult it is to do. One person says it is taking a low estimate of one's merits; another says it is making one's self small. Another says it is a sense of inferiority in the presence of oth-ers. Another says it is a sense of imperfection, or of ill desert. Another says that it is softness, passivity, a willingness to submit.

All of these definitions are proved to be erroneous the moment we carry them into the atmosphere of the New Testament. The hu-mility which Jesus requires of those who follow him is the humility which he had himself, and certainly his humility was not meanness of spirit. There was nothing cringing or crawling in him. When has there walked the earth a man who held his head higher than did he! When has the world known a man of such lofty, sovereign spirit? Nor did he take a low estimate of himself. On the other hand, no man ever estimated himself so highly. Hear him saying to the astounded crowd: "It was said to you by them of old time...but I say to you," thus putting himself higher than Moses. Listen to him as he says: "A greater than Solomon is here" [Luke 11:31 KJV]; "I am the good shepherd" [John 10:14 KJV]; "I am the light of the world" [John 8:12 KJV]; "I am the way, the truth, and the life" [John 14:6 NIV]; "I am from above" [John 8:23 KJV]; "No man knows the Father but the Son"; "No one comes to the Father except through me" [John 14:6 NIV]; "I, if I be lifted up...will draw all men unto me" [John 12:32 KJV]. Certainly humility on the lips of Jesus does not mean a low estimate of one's powers. Let us then come close to him in order to understand just what he means when he says, "I am meek and lowly in heart."

A Childlike Heart

Jesus gave his disciples three great lessons on the subject of humility, and to these I invite your attention. You will find the first of them recorded in Matthew 18:1-4 [NIV]. On a certain occasion Jesus takes a little child, and putting him in the midst, says, "I tell you the truth, unless you change and become like little children, you will never enter the kingdom of heaven. Therefore, whoever humbles himself like this child is the greatest in the kingdom of heaven." The words have been repeated to us so frequently that they fail to surprise the heart. This is one of the great scenes in the history of the world, one of the original scenes. Nothing like it was ever known in the history of Assyria, or of Babylonia, or of Egypt, or of Persia, or of Greece or Rome. It is unique, absolutely original. "Whoever humbles himself like this child"—and what is the crowning characteristic of a little child?

It is teachableness, docility, willingness to learn. A child is eager for knowledge; he is everlastingly asking questions; he is always bent on investigation; he pries into everything. He wants to go to the roots of everything. He always wants you to tell him one more story; he will wear a half dozen grown people out simply by the questions which he asks, so hungry is he for knowledge. This teachableness is humility.

Not only is he free from self-sufficiency, but he is free from vanity. A little child is not vain of the belongings of its parents. He cares nothing for diamonds or silks, brownstone or carriages. He plays with perfect contentment with a child in the street whose parents have no carriages and who are too poor to own diamonds. Free from vanity, he also knows nothing of ambition, nothing of social aspirations. Place before him the queen of England and his own mother, and he will choose his mother every time, though she be nothing but a washerwoman—so simple, so human, so beautiful is the heart of a child. It is this characteristic of the child heart that Jesus loves.

> **He cannot live without prayer. Prayer is the language of humility.**

It was because the Pharisees did not have it that he criticized them and condemned them. They were not teachable; they knew everything. Nobody could tell them anything. They were vain; they blew trumpets and called attention to their decorations. They loved salutations. They were ambitious; they were always pushing themselves forward, taking the chief places at the feasts. He could do nothing with them because they were not humble.

Jesus, on the other hand, had the heart of a child. The evangelists do not tell us about the first twelve years of his life, but in imagination we can see him sitting at the feet of his mother drinking in knowledge from her lips. We can see him in the little school in Nazareth, studying, hungry for knowledge. We get just a glimpse of him at the age of twelve, so hungry for knowledge that he will not go home, but lingers behind to ask the big teachers in the Temple just one more question. Always was he teachable. There is no trace of arrogance in him, no spirit of assumption. He is constantly talking to God, asking him questions, praying for new light. He cannot live without prayer. Prayer is the language of humility. When we say that Jesus was a man of prayer, we say he was meek and lowly in heart.

The Humble Servant

Let us now turn to Matthew 20:25-28 [KJV]. His disciples, in spite of all his admonitions and teachings, are filled with the ambitious spirit. They all want to be first. They want to be high up. Two of them ask for chief places in his kingdom. He tells them that he cannot grant their request. When the ten other apostles heard of the request which the two had made, the ten were indignant. This was because they themselves were ambitious—they wanted the places themselves. Jesus calls the Twelve around him and says, "Know that the princes of the Gentiles exercise dominion over them, and they that are great exercise authority upon them. But it shall not be so among you: but whosoever will be great among you, let him be your minister; and whosoever will be chief among you let him be your servant." Here we get another note in the grace of humility. It is not only teachableness, freedom from vanity and ambition, but it is also a willingness to serve.

A humble man is a man who is ready to make himself useful. A man of lowly spirit is a man who will help his brethren, and here again Jesus in substance says, "Come unto me, for I am meek and lowly in heart. Whosoever will be chief among you let him be your servant, even as the Son of Man came not to be ministered unto but to minister, and to give his life as a ransom for many." Does this not paint the picture of his life? As an inspired apostle puts it, "He went about doing good." He never patronized nor looked down. He made himself of no reputation, if only he could help those that needed help.

He did not underestimate his powers, or make himself small, or feel himself to be unworthy; he simply came down to where men were in order to do them good. That is Christian humility.

Delighting in Low Position

The third lesson in humility was given his disciples on the very night of his betrayal, in the upper chamber. You will find the incident recorded in John 13. The disciples are still filled with the ambitious spirit. They have not yet learned the joy of serving, for all have irritated hearts because they have not gotten the places which they wanted, and Jesus, unwilling to allow the feast to go forward, arises from the table, and taking a basin and girding himself with a towel, proceeds to rinse the dust from the disciples' feet. Knowing their dullness of understanding, he goes on to explain the meaning of his action, telling them that, just as he has been willing to do the work of a slave in order to serve them, so they also must be willing to serve one another.

Here, again, we see what humility really is. It is making one's self of no reputation; it is a willingness to come down; it is a delight in rendering service. And why was it that Jesus was able to do this? John gives the explanation in the wonderful words, "Jesus knew...that he had come from God and was returning to God" [John 13:3 NIV]. It was not because he had mean ideas of himself, nor because he desired to make himself small; it was because he knew his divine origin and his divine destiny and was conscious of his lofty position that he was willing to take the basin and the towel and do the work of a slave. This is the secret of humility everywhere and always. A man is never humble except by coming close to God. Only he who is sure of God possesses the secret of humility.

A Renewed Definition

How far Christian humility is removed from the miserable caricature of humility of which we have seen more than enough. Much of the so-called humility of the world is not humility at all. It is a slimy, crawling, despicable, snaky thing, a compound of vanity and false-hood. People who say they do not amount to anything, that they cannot do anything, never speak the truth. They do not try to speak the truth; they know they are not speaking the truth. It is their ego-tism which is masquerading under the form of humility. There is no vainer form of vanity than just that vanity which apes humility.

The humility which Jesus wants, and which he exemplified in his life, is a form of strength. Only the strong man can be really humble. It is willingness to lay aside one's rights; it is a refusal to use one's power; it is a readiness to come down and to make one's self of no reputation. Jesus was always giving up his rights; he was always refus-ing to use his power. Repeatedly he had the opportunity to wreak vengeance on his enemies, but he would not do it because he was so humble. Despite his exalted position, Paul reminds his Philippian con-verts that Jesus "made himself of no reputation and became obedi-ent unto death, even the death of the cross. Wherefore God also hath highly exalted him, and given him a name...that at the name of Jesus every knee should bow...and every tongue confess that Jesus Christ is Lord" [Philippians 2:7-11 KJV].

"A bruised reed shall he not break."
MATTHEW 12:20 KJV

THE PATIENCE OF JESUS

Words are sometimes like stars. You see a star shining in the sky, and to your eye it is a single star. The astronomer then brings his telescope and to your amazement it is not a single star but a double star, two blazing suns united to produce that shining point of light in the blue. Just so there are words which shine like stars in the firmament of speech, single stars they seem until we subject them to scrutiny, when we discover that two meanings burn within the limits of their narrow syllable.

The word "patience" is not a single, but a double, star. First of all it means "calmly waiting for something hoped for." In this sense even the animals are endowed with the virtue of patience. See the cat watching hour after hour, waiting for the appearance of a rat. She scarcely moves a hair and hardly winks an eye, waiting calmly for that happy moment when her victim shall appear. And just that virtue of imperturbable waiting is one of the great virtues of the human soul. Men have it in greater or lesser degrees, and sometimes it mounts to the level of genius.

But this meaning does not exhaust the significance of patience. See a woman tortured by disease. She has been an invalid for years and in all this time she has never cried aloud, never complained, never rebelled against her fate. Here, indeed, we have something different from what we had in the preceding cases—and yet we call this patience, we look upon the woman in admiration, almost in awe, saying, "I never saw such patience in all my life." Or look at a man at the head of a great reformation movement. He is endeavoring to bring to pass some mighty change in church or state or in society, and he has met with opposition at every step. For a while he makes progress, and then the way is blocked. Enemies multiply; friends forsake him; hearts grow cold. He is misunderstood, misrepresented, maligned, and hated, but, nevertheless, he goes bravely on, unsoured by opposition, undaunted by vituperation, never complaining, always hoping, bearing rebuff and reproof and criticism without a whine or a protest. Here again is patience. What is patience here? It is "the uncomplaining endurance of tribulation."

These, then, are the two ideas which burn within the limits of our word "patience." First, it is the calm waiting for something hoped for; second, it is the unruffled endurance of pain and trouble. It is a temper of the soul, a temper that endures, waits, holds on. A person may have one sort of patience and not the other. Would you see patience in both its forms raised to its highest power without a defect and without a flaw, you will find it in Jesus of Nazareth.

Patient Through the Early Years

If patience means the calm waiting for something hoped for, then Jesus had this in a superlative degree. Was any waiting ever like his? He waited in a little country town in Galilee for thirty years before he entered into the work he felt God had given him to do. We do not always stop to ask ourselves how much this must have cost him. Think of what delay must have meant to Jesus. How his blood must have boiled in little sleepy Nazareth as he dreamed of the mighty things which ought to be done and which he felt he could do in the great arena! As man after man brushed by him on his way to success and renown, his soul must have been agitated. He, too, must have felt the fever to hasten on. Think of what his dream was, and you will understand how it must have tugged at him and made the years seem interminable in drowsy, prosaic Nazareth. But he waited. At twenty-one he said, *Not yet.* At twenty-five, *Not yet.* At twenty-eight, *Not yet.* It is in the twenties that the blood is hottest and the soul is most eager to get on. Through all the blazing years of youth, Jesus waited in Nazareth. It was not until he was in his thirtieth year that he said to himself, *The time has come.*

A man at thirty is more than one-third of the way through life, and since Jesus has so much to do, certainly now that he has been baptized, he will plunge into his work with alacrity and push his projects with a vigor which will startle his contemporaries. Not so. He will calmly meditate on the best ways of helping his day and generation. The leaders of the people were looking for a man who would imitate the methods of the men who had hitherto proved themselves

> He demanded much of his disciples, but he did not demand it all at once.

master of the destinies of nations. Jesus listened to these voices; they came up from all directions, thundering in his ears. In imagination he saw himself on the top of a lofty mountain with the kingdoms of the world lying stretched out below him. He saw how he might gain possession of them by adopting methods employed by those who had lived before his day.

But having considered the whole situation he said, "No, I will not do what others have done; I will choose the slow and toilsome way. I will not cut the knot; I will untie it. I will not push the world; I will draw it. I will not subdue the world by military methods; I will heal it by the sympathy of human hearts." With this conviction firmly established in his soul, he began his ministry in Galilee. To the men who stood around him, he was always slow. "Why don't you go on? Why don't you hurry? Why don't you bring things to pass? Why don't you say everything you are going to say? Why don't you do everything you are going to do? Why don't you do it now?"—these were the questions which were thrown at him by friends and enemies all along the way. But when they urged him to hurry, his reply was, "Are there not twelve hours in the day?" [John 11:9 KJV] or "My hour has not yet come" [John 2:4 NASB]. And instead of setting all the land afire, he tried, so it seemed, to suppress himself, to hold his disciples back, to keep his name from becoming glorious. When he healed sick men, he said to them, "Tell no man."

When his disciples saw him all radiant on the mountain, he cautioned them to keep still. The result was that, at the end of his life, he had made only one hundred and twenty disciples. What a pitiful outcome of a life so arduous, of work so strenuous and so unceasing! But the sight of a hundred and twenty men did not daunt him. He died with contentment in his heart. "Be of good cheer; I have overcome the world" [John 16:33 KJV]. When? Not then. Nevertheless, he has the tone of victory in his voice, knowing that, in spite of all the obstacles, delays and retrogressions, the outcome is absolutely certain. Before Pontius Pilate, the Roman procurator, he says, "To this end was I born and for this cause came I into the world, that I should bear witness unto the truth" [John 18:37 KJV]. He did his work and died. The progress has been slow, but his patient heart is still untroubled.

Patient with Enemies and Friends

But this does not exhaust the patience of Jesus. The way of a reformer is never smooth, and the way which Jesus traveled was the thorniest which human feet have ever trod. It was literal truth that he came unto his own and his own received him not, that the light shone in the darkness but the darkness comprehended it not. With a love that caused his heart to glow, he knocked at the door in Jerusalem, but the men who kept the door refused to open it. He knocked at the door in Nazareth, and the door was opened then shut in his face.

He traveled throughout Galilee, and in city after city he met with repulse; but he was never discouraged; he never complained.

This Man of Galilee knew little but misunderstanding and ingratitude and criticism and abuse; but he never complained, and at the end of the day, he was as sweet as at dawn. Long before he came, somebody had said that when the supreme man arrived, he would submit to tribulation without complaining. As men looked upon this Man of Galilee, they were reminded of the great line of the prophet, "As a sheep before her shearers is silent, so he did not open his mouth" [Isaiah 53:7 NIV].

And if Jesus was patient with his enemies, he was equally patient with his friends—and probably his friends tried him no less sorely than his enemies. His friends did not understand him. His own mother and brothers were not in sympathy with him. The disciples to whom he gave himself with a devotion that has never been equaled were constantly failing to catch the import of the things he told them. They were slow and stupid, petty and selfish, unable to take in the great things he had to say—but he was patient with them.

Even on the last night of his earthly life, when he met his disciples in a private house in Jerusalem to have a last talk with them, they quarreled among themselves as to their places at the table. But even this brings from him no more than an affectionate rebuke. He simply takes a basin of water and performs the work which was ordinarily performed by slaves, rinsing the dust from their unsandalled feet—by this act teaching what he had been trying to teach them from the beginning: that he who would be greatest must be the servant of all.

There is a beautiful quotation in the Old Testament which the apostle Matthew has put at the center of his Gospel, throwing a flood of light upon the impression which Jesus made upon those who came nearest to him. After he had vanished from their sight, the beauty of his character came up before them as they had never been able to see it in the days of his humiliation, and among the beautiful portraits which men in preceding generations had sketched of an ideal character, Matthew felt that not one more fully portrayed Jesus of Nazareth than this one: "A bruised reed shall he not break, and the smoking flax shall he not quench" [Isaiah 42:3 KJV]. This was his temper whether he was dealing with foes or friends.

He demanded much of his disciples, but he did not demand it all at once. He kept saying that if a man has even a little faith, even so small as a grain of mustard seed, he has enough to start with, and by means of this, he will be able to work wonders. Great men have oftentimes been notoriously impatient with their weaker and more incompetent brethren; strong themselves, they could not sympathize with weakness; clear in their own conceptions, they could not endure the stupidity of those who floundered in mist and fog. The bruised reed they had no use for; the smoking wick they despised and quenched.

But the patient Man of Galilee had a temper altogether different. He sympathized with weakness; he was considerate of mental dullness; he was long-suffering in the presence of moral awkwardness. Even a bruised reed he would not break, and a smoking wick he would coax back into flame.

The Long View

And ever since Jesus lived and taught, men have loved to think that God is patient. To every follower of Jesus, the Almighty is a long-suffering God. He has vast plans running through the ages, and He is willing to wait for their fulfillment. Men look around them at the woe and havoc, the suffering and the tragedy, and say, "How could God ever make a world like this? How can He endure it to have these things go on?" They do not understand that He is patient, infinitely patient, and is willing to wait until human hearts surrender, and by their obedience, bring the long and bitter night to an end. Not only does He wait, but He also suffers indignity at our hands without blazing up in anger and consuming us. We may be ungrateful, insolent, irreverent, rebellious; we may refuse to do the things He asks us to do, and persist in doing the things that are contrary to His will; we may injure ourselves and hurt others; nevertheless He will not strike us down. He will give us yet another day, and still another, saying, "Perhaps tomorrow the sin will be repented of and the prodigal will come home."

"Fear not."
LUKE 5:10 KJV

THE COURAGE OF JESUS

He who speaks of courage speaks of a live subject. It is a virtue which everybody admires and which everybody has admired from the beginning. There has never been a nation which did not admire courageous men. When we deal, therefore, with courage, we are dealing with a virtue which is not peculiar to any race, or confined to any generation, or deemed a virtue by any one religion. It is one of the elemental tempers of the human spirit, one of the foundation stones in the great structure of character.

When we come, therefore, to the study of the ideal man, we might expect to find him giving us a wonderful exhibition of courage. And this is indeed what we find: In Jesus of Nazareth we find bravery at its best, courage at its loftiest, heroism at its pinnacle.

Ordinary Courage

There are different kinds of courage. There is a courage which we may call physical. It runs in the blood; it is a kind of instinct. This sort of courage is not peculiar to man; it is possessed also by the animals. The bulldog has it, and so also has the weasel. It is possessed by man in all the stages of his development. It is an aversion to danger, a contempt for suffering and for death. But the courage of Jesus was not this. His was the courage of the mind, the heroism of the heart. It was a sober and reasoned thing. He deliberately counted the cost and paid it.

Nor was his courage military. Military courage is the most common of all forms of courage in the world, and one of the earliest developed. Military courage is the courage which the soldier has in the time of battle. In time of battle men move in masses; the very momentum of the movement carries them onward. The courage of our Lord was not military; it was the courage which manifested itself in isolation. There was nobody to march with him. He marched alone.

There is also such a thing as occasional courage—courage that is born of some feverish moment, drawn from the heart by some overwhelming disaster. This is the courage which we see displayed in time of a great fire, or of a great flood, or of a great wreck on the sea. This courage is indeed sublime, but it is not equal to the courage of repose. Disaster heats the blood and kindles a fire in the mind which makes it easy for the soul to dare great things; but the courage of Jesus of Nazareth was the courage of the quiet and commonplace days, courage that had to be manifested hour by hour along the dusty road when there was nothing to heat the blood or stir the mind to lofty moods.

Courage Through Alienation

If you were to paint Jesus as a hero, in what situation would you sketch him? Would you think of him on that great day on which he cleansed the Temple, driving out the cattle, overturning the tables of the money-changers, saying to sellers of doves, "Get these out of here"? [John 2:16 NIV]. Would you paint him as he appeared when in the streets of Jerusalem he stood up and faced his implacable foes, the Scribes and Pharisees, and hurled at them sentences which, at the distance of nineteen hundred years, still smoke like thunderbolts? Or would you paint him as he came from the Garden of Gethsemane and startled the band of men who have come to arrest him by say-ing, "I am the man you seek"? Or would you picture him going to Golgotha saying to the women who bewailed his fate, "Weep not for me, but weep for yourselves, and for your children"? [Luke 23:28 KJV]. All these situations, I admit, are picturesque and thrilling. Every reader of the New Testament catches them up and holds them forever in his memory. In each one of them we see heroism in a high and lovely form, but these are not the scenes to which I call your attention at the present moment.

Would you ask me to give you an illustration of the courage of Jesus' heart, I would take you first of all to Nazareth on that day on which, for the first time, he announced his mission to the men and women who had known him from boyhood. It was necessary for him to say things which would offend, and he said them. He was to preach the truth, but he could not preach the truth without cutting across the grain of the prejudices of these people. He went calmly on-ward, however, and preached the truth. To estrange the hearts of those who have known and es-teemed us for many years, to cut one's self off from the respect and sympathy and love of those in whose friendship we have

> His was the courage of the mind, the heroism of the heart. It was a sober and reasoned thing. He deliberately counted the cost and paid it.

found solace and delight—that is hard indeed. And that is what Jesus did on that awful day in Nazareth. By the simple speaking of the truth, he alienated from himself the minds and hearts of the people in whose midst he had grown to manhood and whose high regard had been one of the most valuable of all his earthly treasures.

He was a courageous man that day, and equally courageous was he in the streets of Capernaum when he talked to that crowd of five thousand men whom he had just fed previously in the desert. He came into the world to bear witness to the truth, but men were not willing to receive it. At the beginning of his address everyone was enthusiastic, but as he spoke, the great crowd began to melt away. The five thousand decreased to three thousand; the three thousand sank to two thousand; the two thousand became one thousand; the one thousand fell to five hundred; the five hundred to one hundred; the one hundred to fifty; the fifty to twenty-five; and these at last became twenty; the twenty dwindled to fifteen; and at last only twelve men stood beside him, and these twelve had such doleful, wavering faces that he said to them, "You do not want to leave too, do you?" [John 6:67 NIV]. What is there harder in this world than that? A religious teacher finds his joy in the ears and hearts of those who hear him. To hold them, to teach them, to inspire them—this is indeed his glory, his all. But to teach the truth and go on teaching it even though the congregation grows less and less and less, that requires the forthputting of the very highest temper of the soul. It was just that kind of courage which Jesus had. The courage which he manifested in Capernaum was manifested everywhere.

It is not an easy thing to offend society and to offend it in such a way as to lose caste and standing. The people in Jesus' day were great sticklers for forms of fasting. Jesus minimized the value of them. They were exceedingly scrupulous in regard to sabbatical laws. Jesus could not keep them; he did not believe in keeping them. They were punctilious in regard to the number of times they washed their hands before they sat down to eat. Jesus had no time for such elaborate foolery. The best people of his day divided things into clean and unclean, people into clean and unclean—Jesus could pay no attention to these distinctions. All men were his brethren, and so he associated with people who had lost caste. By so doing he lost his own reputation. He went contrary to the established usages of the best society of his day; he trampled on conventionalities which were counted sacred as the law of the Eternal. And the result was [that] he was suspected, shunned and abhorred.

But he did even more than this: He surrendered the good opinion which many of the people had formed of him. When he first appeared, the air was filled with applause; men looked upon him as the promised Messiah. The land blazed with enthusiasm. The people had certain ideals, and Jesus could not form to them. They had fixed ideas, and Jesus could not carry them out. He threw cold water upon these fires of enthusiasm, and they died down lower and lower until at last there was nothing but a great stretch of smoldering ashes; and he stood in the center of the ashes the most forsaken and hated of men. It takes tremendous courage to lay aside one's reputation and also to forego the bliss of popular applause. But he did a braver thing even than this: He gave up the good opinion of the best people of his day. He was reverent, religious, sensitive, but there were certain things it was necessary for him to say because they were true things—and he said them. By saying them he exposed himself to the charge of being a blasphemer, but he said them. He was willing to do his duty even though by the doing of it, he won for himself the ignominy of being counted a blasphemer, a lunatic and a traitor. Only the very loftiest heroism can meet such a test as that. But we have not yet reached the zenith.

If it is difficult for a man to withstand his enemies, much more difficult is it for him to withstand his friends. There are many men who can resist the people who are opposed to them who cannot withstand the opinions and wishes of their friends. Many of us can pour denunciation on the men who hate us, but we succumb at once to the gracious words of those who wish us well. Peter was Jesus' dearest friend; but when Peter on a certain occasion says to him, "Far be it from thee, Lord; this shall not be unto thee," quick as a flash the reply comes, "Get thee behind me, Satan" [Matthew 16:22-23 KJV]. Also James and John present what seems to them a most reasonable request and Jesus says, "I cannot grant this." Judas was one of the most trusted of the apostolic company—so trusted that he was made the treasurer of the band—but Jesus, by the simple telling of the truth and the living of a perfect life, estranged the affections of this man until at last he became his betrayer. Many of you have courage sufficient to stand against your enemies, but how many of you can resist the influence and wishes of your friends?

A Lifetime of Courage

But if you want illustrations of the courage of Jesus, you must take the entire New Testament, for all the Gospels are a portrait of a hero. The story of Jesus' life is the most heroic record ever written, and any man who wishes to increase the bravery of his heart must read this book day and night. See him as he sets his face steadfastly to go to Jerusalem, where he knows they are going to scourge him and spit upon him and kill him. His friends endeavor to dissuade him; they strive to hold him back. He keeps steadily on, knowing that at Jerusalem he will give his life as a ransom for many. Perhaps you have engaged in some reform and have been misrepresented and abused. You have turned away, saying, "I am tired; I am sick." Why do men talk thus? Because they are cowards. Only cowards surrender; only cowards get tired and sick. Jesus steadfastly set his face to go to Jerusalem and never turned back until he reached the cross. See him as he goes onward, trampling on all the precious things of earth, putting under his feet the ambitions by which the hearts of other men are fired, trampling into the dust the prizes and the joys of life. Make out a list of the things which you count most valuable and worthwhile, and you will see that Jesus placed every one of them beneath his feet. With the tread of a conqueror, he goes on to his death, saying, "I do always those things that are pleasing unto Him" [John 8:29 KJV].

17

"And when he had looked round
about on them with anger…"

MARK 3:5 KJV

THE INDIGNATION OF JESUS

There are certain moods and feelings which we are reluctant to ascribe to Jesus because they are so common and so human. Characteristics which are conspicuous and disconcerting in ourselves, we do not readily associate with him. For instance, was it possible for Jesus to be angry? If it was, he was amazingly like ourselves. The humblest and least gifted of us are adept in the realm of indignation. Our capacity for wrath was manifested in us early, and we have developed it by constant use. No emotion is more nearly universal, and none is more easily aroused. The very universality of the experience makes us reluctant to attribute it to one who is, at so many points, above us, and whose life, however like our own, has in it so many things which are unique.

Moreover, anger is associated in our mind with infirmity. Much of our own anger has been worldly. It has been a boiling of the blood, full of sound and fury, having no ethical significance. Sometimes it has been a burst of petulance, an explosion of nervous energy, a sort of madness bordering on the frontiers of insanity. While the fever was upon us we felt our wrath was justifiable, but on the cooling of the blood we repented in sackcloth and ashes. We have also noticed what anger does for others. It has not escaped us that when men and women are angry, they usually make fools of themselves. This fact has made a deep impression on us. Most of the indignation which we have known has been so childish or so brutish, so full of fury and of bitterness, that we find it hard to give it place in the experience of a strong and holy man.

So prone is anger to mix itself with base and unlovely elements, and so frequently does it stir up the mud at the bottom of the soul, that it has been often classed among the vices as a passion which is always ignoble and therefore to be condemned, resisted, strangled. It was thus that the Stoics taught, contending that ever to be moved by anger is a sign of weakness and unworthy of a mature man.

A New View of Anger

It is because of the assumption that anger is, in its essence, sinful that many persons find it impossible to think of Jesus in an angry mood. When the New Testament says that he was angry, they glide over the sentence hurriedly and breathe more freely when they have come out again into a paragraph which portrays his tenderness and love. Once you decide that anger is a sinful or an animal passion, you must deny it a place in the portrait of an ideal man.

But the evangelists were not Stoics, and they were not handicapped by the notions which bewilder us. They felt that they must write down clearly what they saw and heard, and prompted thus to tell a round, unvarnished tale, they do not hesitate to inform us that Jesus sometimes blazed with anger. The blast of his scorn was so hot that it frightened and scorched those on whom it fell. They tell us that it was inhumanity and insincerity which always kindled his heart to furnace heat. When he saw men—ordained religious leaders of the people—more interested in their petty regulations than in the welfare of their fellowmen, his eyes burned with holy fire. Those who were present never forgot the flash of his eye as he slowly looked round upon the pettifoggers whose hardness of heart he held in abhorrence. He despised the lying superstitions which had accumulated around the idea of death, and loathed the dramatic performances which attended the burial of the dead. The hollow howlings of paid mourners in the presence of the holy mystery of death aroused his soul to indignant protest. Any darkening of the world by cruelty or craft brought his soul to its feet fiery-eyed and defiant.

He was angered by the desecration of the Temple. The sordid wretches who cared nothing for anthems and prayers and everything for money, kindled a fire in him which well-nigh consumed him. The miscreants who fled before him had never seen such a flame as darted from his eyes. That a building constructed for the purpose of adorning the name of God should be converted into a market was so abhorrent to his great soul that he was swept onward into action which astounded his disciples and which has been, to many, a scandal ever since. No one can understand the cleansing of the Temple who has never experienced the force and heat of righteous indignation.

There are many sentences from his lips which, after the lapse of nineteen hundred years, still burn with fervent heat. Who can read the parable of Dives and Lazarus without feeling the fire of a holy scorn? Who can read the denunciation of the Pharisees without realizing that he is in the presence of a volcano belching molten lava? No one could speak language like that which the evangelists have recorded who was not capable of tremendous indignation. It is a wrath which leaps beyond the wrath of man. It is the very wrath of God Himself. One of the purposes

> The blast of his scorn was so hot that it frightened and scorched those on whom it fell.

of the New Testament is to give us a new revelation of anger. Take away Jesus' capacity for indignation, and you destroy the Jesus of the Gospels. His blazing wrath is one of the most glorious features of his character. Had he been less emotional, he would not have stirred men as he did. Had his passion been less intense, the world would never have called him "Master."

Two Sides of a Coin

Here, then, we have in Jesus what seems to some a contradiction. He is a Lamb, and at the same time he is the Lion of the Tribe of Judah. He caresses like a mother, and he also strikes like a thunderbolt. He is tender, but he is also terrible; he is loving, but he also smites with a blow which crushes. How can we reconcile the indignation of Jesus with his love? Nothing is easier. His indignation is the creation of his love. His wrath proceeds from his holiness. His mercy would have no meaning were it not for his immeasurable capacity for anger. Take away his indignation, and you destroy the basis of his holiness, his righteousness, his mercy, and his love.

Love and indignation are not antagonists or rivals. They ever go together, each one unable to live without the other. Only those who have never loved have difficulty in understanding the heart's capacity for wrath. Did you ever see a lover stand calm-eyed and gentle-tempered in the presence of the villain who had dared insult the queen of his heart? When, since the world began, has love ever maintained a quiet pulse in the presence of the assailant of the loved one? A mother, all gentleness and sweetness as she moves among her children, passes into an avenging fury in the face of a foe who attempts to harm them. The dimensions of her indignation will be determined by the depth and heat of her love. It is the hottest love which, when enlisted in the welfare of others, scorches opposing forces to cinders. The power of loving and the power of hating must always go together. There is right and there is

> The thought of evil men leading innocent souls to sin converted him into a furnace of fire.

wrong, the first must be approved; the second must be condemned. The condemnation must not be cold, but vehement. It must carry with it all the energy of the soul. It must have at the heart of it that heavenly fire which is known on earth as indignation.

In Jesus, then, we see what a normal man is and feels. He is full-orbed, complete. He gives sweep to every passion of the soul. He will not admit that in the garden of the heart there are any plants which the Heavenly Father has planted which ought to be rooted up. All the impulses, desires and passions with which the Almighty has endowed us have a mission to perform, and life's task is not to strangle them, but to train them for their work.

Jesus was angry, but he did not sin. Anger, because of its heat, readily passes beyond its appointed limits. Like all kinds of fire, it is dangerous and difficult to control. But Jesus controlled it. "Thus far," he said, "and no farther." No sinful element mingled in that indignation which burned with a white and resistless heat. The irritation which we so often feel, the exasperation which lacerates and rends the heart, the bitterness of which we are ashamed—all these were absent from Jesus' anger. His wrath was the hottest ever known upon our earth, but the heart in which it burned was sinless.

Ungodly Anger

Our anger is frequently a manifestation of our selfishness. We become indignant over trifles. The street-car does not stop; somebody carelessly knocks off our hat; or a servant disappoints us, and we are all aflame. Our comfort has been molested, our rights have been entrenched upon, or our dignity has been affronted, and we are downright mad. Ravelings and shavings can set us blazing. But in the presence of gigantic outrages perpetrated on the helpless and the weak, some of us are as calm as a summer morning. Evil men do not make us angry unless they interfere with our own personal affairs. If they wrong others, we will make excuses for them, and cover them all over with the down of extenuating syllables, saying, "Poor men, they are more sinned against than sinning. They are the products of the age, the victims of the system," and thus do we take from guilt its heinousness by the flattering smile of a placid face.

Our indignation, then, is quite different from that of Jesus. His anger never had its roots in selfishness. When men abused him, he was unruffled. When they lied about him, his pulse was not quickened. When they nailed his hands to the cross, no trace of anger darkened his face. His calm lips kept on praying, "Forgive them, for they know not what they do" [Luke 23:34 KJV]. It was when he saw his brother men abused that his great soul rose in wrath. The more helpless the person who was mistreated, the hotter was the fire of his indignation. Against rich people who imposed upon the poor, and against clever people who took advantage of the ignorant, and against strong people who mistreated the weak, and against crafty people who laid traps for the innocent, his soul blazed with a heat which became an imperishable an awe-inspiring memory in the apostolic church. It was when he saw cruelty perpetrated on the defenseless that his indignation rose to the fury of a tempest. The thought of evil men leading innocent souls to sin converted him into a furnace of fire. What a whirlwind of flame sweeps through a sentence like this: "And if anyone causes one of these little ones who believe in me to sin, it would be better for him to be thrown into the sea with a large millstone tied around his neck" [Mark 9:42 NIV]. Tender, indeed, must have been the heart from which could come such forked lightnings!

If, then, we have ever been scandalized by the account of Jesus' indignation, we should examine ourselves and find out why we shrink from the thought that a man like him should burn with anger. Whenever we find in Jesus a word or deed which seems to us to be a departure from what we conceive to be the standard of absolute righteousness, it is well to pause and study our standards of righteousness afresh, for it may be that what we conceive to be a defect in him may reveal to us a limitation in ourselves. If we find fault with him because he blazed with anger, it may be that our criticism springs from blood which has become impoverished. If we fail to burn in the presence of cruelty and injustice, it is because the higher faculties of the soul have become atrophied by sin. If wood does not burn, it is because it is green or rotten. If hearts do not burn with holy fire against wicked men and their wicked deeds, it is because the heart is too undeveloped to feel what hearts were meant to feel, or because the core of the heart has been eaten out by the base practices of a godless life.

Righteous Indignation

Indifference to wrong-doing is always a sign of moral deterioration. If we do not flame against villainy, it is because there is so much of the villain in ourselves. We would despise graft with a consuming detestation if our own palms were not so itching. The healthy soul resents and resists every form of wrong. The unspoiled heart goes out like a man in wrath against the forces of iniquity. Nothing is more needed in our day than enlarged capacity for moral indignation. Nothing so clears the atmosphere as the heat of hearts heated by holy anger. There are evils so gigantic and so deeply rooted that nothing less than a thunderstorm will overwhelm them. Bad men will abound more and more unless good men hurl thunderbolts.

Criminals become brazen; wrong-doers walk insolently; and rascals take possession of high places until good men, aflame with indignation, arise and sweep them from the seats of power. Society would be cleansed of much of its pollution if we had more men and women capable of becoming genuinely angry. Let us pray, then, every day that a new indignation may sweep through the world. It is the devil's trick to keep good men from becoming angry. Not only are we permitted as Christians to be angry, but it is our duty, on occasion, to allow this billow of fire to roll through the soul. Martin Luther is not the only man who has worked better when he was angry, and many of us limp to our task because we have lost one of the elements of moral power.

'Exact Representation of His Being'

In the indignation of Jesus we shed light upon the character of God. This man's anger flows from a fountain in the heart of the Eternal. The "wrath of the Lamb" is, as we have been often reminded, a figure of speech, but like all biblical figures of speech, it is a window opening out on the infinite. The anger of Jesus is a revelation of the anger of God. It is significant that it is the beloved disciple and the man to whom tradition has ascribed a heart unusually loving and tender, who has most to say about the "wrath of the Lamb." As he brooded over the years of his interactions with Jesus, there was one trait which rose before him again and again, and that was the anger of Jesus. When he speaks of it, it is always with syllables which hush the heart. The man who declares that "God is love" is the man who exhorts us to flee from the "wrath of the Lamb."

The New Testament is a glorious book! Its lines are straight; its judgment is fine; it rings true. It is absolutely free from sentimentalism. It has no sickly fondness for evil people. It does not deal in excuses and in extenuations. It has no abnormal tenderness. The world is full of sentimentalists—men and women who gush about love and who do not truly know what love is. After listening to their flimsy talk, it is refreshing to get into a book where every bad deed is held up to scorn and every evil man, if unrepentant, is overwhelmed with shame. Nowhere in the Gospels is there a soft or flabby thought, a doughy or mushy feeling. All is high and straight and fine and firm and true. Under such a sky, life becomes august, solemn, beautiful. It is worthwhile to strive, to work, to suffer. One feels sure that God is in His heaven, and that though wickedness may flourish for a season, God's heart burns with quenchless fire against it, and that, at the end of the days, every impure man and every cruel man and every man who loves and makes a lie, will find himself outside the city whose streets are gold and whose gates are pearl.

18

"Hallowed be thy name."

MATTHEW 6:9 KJV

THE REVERENCE OF JESUS

No analysis of the character of Jesus would be complete which failed to recognize his reverence. It is one of the traits which contribute most largely to his loveliness, a characteristic which attracts the notice of every observing mind. To write a definition of reverence is not easy. There are some things which the heart can sense, but which the intellect cannot easily define. We know what reverence is, and yet we stumble in trying to define it. It is "respect, regard, esteem and honor"; yes, and it is more than these. Those thin and pallid syllables do not express all which the heart feels when the word "reverence" is spoken. The basis of reverence is respect or honor, but it is respect or honor working with atypical energy. It is a deep movement of the soul. It is respect or honor squared or cubed.

And then again there is an elevation in the word "reverence" which respect and esteem do not have. It is respect and esteem moving at high altitudes. It is one of the loftiest of all the emotions of the soul, and that is why it eludes us when we try to capture it in the meshes of a definition. What is it? It is homage and deference and devotion, yes, and something more. It is awe and fear and adoration; yes, but even these do not tell the full-rounded story. The fact is, reverence is a complex emotion, made up of mingled feelings of the soul. There is in it respect and also affection and also fear, and along with these, an abiding consciousness of dependence. There is probably no expression which defines what we mean by reverence so well as the Old Testament phrase, "The fear of the Lord."

From Old Testament to New

The wise men of Israel were convinced that the fear of the Lord is the beginning of wisdom. Their effort was to make men conscious of the existence of a God of infinite power and wisdom and goodness. He was the High and Holy One who inhabits eternity and is, therefore, not to be approached carelessly or thought of lightly. The Temple in Jerusalem was built in such a way as to establish the fear of the Lord in the hearts of the people. Its architecture was continually reminding them that to be reverent is to be wise. Into the outer courts of the Temple every Hebrew might go; into the inner court or holy place only one man was permitted to make his way, and that man only on one great day of the year. In this way the cardinal truth was proclaimed that God is majestic and holy and can be approached only by a humble and prostrate heart. This fear of the Lord was mighty in Jesus. God was continually before his eyes. His soul was pervaded with the sense of His presence, and all that he said and did was bathed in an atmosphere created by this consciousness of the fellowship and favor of the Eternal.

To illustrate this is not easy. Jesus' entire life is an illustration of it. One cannot pick out isolated words or acts and hold them up, saying, "Behold, how reverent he was!" A man cannot be reverent at intervals. He must be reverent all the time or not at all. If he is reverent on Monday and not on Tuesday, then his Monday reverence was a pretense and a sham. Reverence is not a vesture which can be put on and laid off—it runs in the very blood of the soul. It is impossible to localize it. It is, rather, an atmosphere in which the personality is enveloped. It is a settled habit of the spirit, a fixed attitude of the heart, an unchanging trend of all the currents of the being toward God. No matter what Jesus is saying or doing, we feel we are in the presence of a reverential man. Would you see illustrations of his reverence, read the Gospels!

Reverent Prayer

The earnestness with which he was always pleading for reverence in others is proof that in him reverence was a divine and indispensable possession. He could not have so loved it in others had he not possessed it himself. "When you pray, say, 'Our Father, hallowed be thy name.'" Probably no other words in the Lord's prayer have been so frequently slurred and overlooked as "hallowed be thy name." We slide over them as though they were only a parenthesis and hasten on to ask for bread and deliverance from our greatest foe. But Jesus is careful to place this petition at the very forefront of all our praying. Unless this desire is uppermost in our heart, we are not in the mood of prayer. If our first thought is of ourselves and not of God, then we are not praying after the fashion of Jesus. When he tells us to put this petition first, it is because he always put it first himself. It was his supreme ambition that his Father's name should be kept beautiful and holy. "When you pray, then," he said to his disciples, "pray that God's name may be consecrated, reverenced, kept holy; hedge it from the contaminating influences of an evil world; separate it from all other names which the lips speak or the mind thinks." Any low or unworthy thought of God was, to Jesus' mind, abhorrent and degrading. Living always with an eye single to the glory of God, he urged men everywhere so to speak and act and live that others, seeing their good works, might glorify their Father in heaven.

Heavenly Perspective

Holding God continually before his eyes, he saw everything in relation to the Eternal. His respect for men was due, not to what men were in themselves, but to what they were in the eyes of God. They were God's children, and therefore, no matter how poor or degraded, they were worthy of respect and honor. Any cruelty in word or inhumanity in action toward a human being caused the heart of Jesus to flash fire, because such treatment of God's children was, in his mind, an insult to God Himself. His reverence for his Father made the whole world holy, and because of his adoration for the Creator, he could not turn his back upon any created being. "Honor all men" was one of the earliest exhortation of the apostles. It had its roots running down into Jesus' immeasurable reverence for God.

How careful he was for the fair name of his Father is illustrated in what he says in regard to oaths. The religious leaders of his day had a certain form of reverence, but it was circumscribed and shallow. They reverenced the letters which spelled God's name so highly that they would never take them upon their lips, but they had no hesitation in filling the empty spaces with other words. If they would not swear in the name of God, they would fill their oaths with the names of things which God had made. Jesus' reverence for his Father was so intense that it extended also to the things created by his Father. The Jews were in the habit of swearing by heaven, but this to Jesus was profane because heaven was made by God. They sometimes swore by the earth, but this was to him also shocking because the earth belongs to God. Sometimes they swore by Jerusalem, but this also could not be permitted, for it was a city dear to God. If they swore by their own heads, they were also in the wrong, for their head was created by the Almighty. Here is, indeed, a sensitive heart. He feels so keenly the majesty and dignity of the Eternal Father that all created things shine in the reflected glory of His face, and therefore nothing is to be treated irreverently, dragged down into vulgarity or converted into a joke.

His reverence for the Temple was unfailing. Every stone in it spoke to him of God, and every ceremony celebrated within its courts had in it a meaning which soothed and comforted his heart. Any desecration of a building constructed to promote God's glory was to him horrible and unendurable. It was in this building that eyes were to be opened and hearts cleansed to behold the King in His beauty. Around it clustered sacred associations and sweet memories of many years. It was to Jesus, indeed, a holy place. But not so to many of his countrymen. In the process of moral degradation, reverence is one of the first of the virtues to disappear. It is a flower of paradise which cannot blossom in the chill atmosphere of sordidness and vulgarity. The love of money had eaten out the hearts of many of Jesus' countrymen. They cared more for gain than they did for God.

Caring nothing for God, why should they care for God's temple? They converted the temple courts into a marketplace and drowned the anthems and the prayers with the clink of money and the bellowing of steers. Jesus could not endure it. Other men had endured it—he could not. Irreverence is a sword through the heart of a reverent man. Never did Jesus show such a tempest of emotion as in the cleansing of the Temple. To the onlookers he seemed to be beside himself. He became all at once an avenging fury, and before the miscreants knew what was happening, their coins were rolling over the temple floor, and their flocks and herds were in the street. The explanation of the tempest lies in these three words: "my Father's house." It was not an ordinary house. It was the house of God. It was built for God's worship. It was a shrine for the adoring heart. It was intended to be a solace for men's woes and troubles, the very gate of Heaven. "Get these out of here! How dare you turn my Father's house into a market!" [John 2:16 NIV]. It was his reverence which kindled a fire in his eyes and gave his words an energy which pierced like daggers.

Reverent Remembrances

Jesus believed in the worship of God. He was careful always to maintain the ceremonies which nourish and guard the high sentiments of the heart. His attitude to ritual has often been misunderstood by persons who, glancing at the surface, have not caught the significance of what he did. He made unrelenting war upon the Pharisees who were the anointed custodians of the religion of their day. He criticized their ways of fasting and giving and praying and dressing and held up their entire life to condemnation. And because of this, it has been sometimes said that Jesus did not believe in ceremonies.

> This fear of the Lord was mighty in Jesus. God was continually before his eyes.

This is an error. Jesus did not believe in ritualism—the corpse of ceremony, ceremony after the spirit of life has gone out of it.

Jesus hated death wherever he found it. He hated it most of all in the form of worship. Worship is the body in which reverence enshrines itself. So long as the spirit of reverence lives, the worship is meaningful and beautiful; but when the spirit disappears, then the worship becomes demoralizing and corrupting. The worship of the Pharisees sorely lacked the spirit of adoration. It was cut and dried, dead, mechanical, without a heart and without a soul, and therefore odious to God and all right-thinking men. Reverence is beautiful and renders beautiful whatever form it chooses in which to express itself; but when reverence dies, then the forms of reverence become corpse-like and contaminate all who handle them.

Jesus believed in ceremonies. They are, when rightly used, the conservators of life. If you want to keep alive the spirit of courtesy and politeness, then do not cast away the forms of politeness and courtesy. If you wish to keep the fires of love burning, do not banish the forms in which love delights to express itself. If you desire to maintain the spirit of friendship, be sure you treasure all its forms. He was a wise man who advised us to keep our friendships in repair, and they who do not do this find in the end that their friendships have decayed and passed away. Would you keep alive the spirit of reverence, then make use of the rituals which are best adapted to feed and develop that spirit in the soul.

Jesus made fierce war on ritualism, but he ever was a scrupulous observer of ritual. He was always in the Synagogue on the Sabbath day. He followed faithfully the order of the service. He repeated the prayers; he sang the psalms; and he listened to the reading of the Scriptures. When he fed the five thousand men on the other side of Jordan, he was careful to return thanks to God before the meal proceeded. When he stood at the grave of Lazarus, he first looked to God in prayer before he spoke the words, "Come out!" [John 11:43 NIV]. In the upper chamber he observed the Passover, omitting nothing from the ritual—sacred because transmitted through so many generations. The soul of Jesus was reverent. He found it easy to bend the knee. It was natural for him to look up. He looked into his Father's face, saying at every step, "Lo, I come to do Thy will, O God!"

Increasing Irreverence

Here, then we have a virtue upon whose beauty we should often fix our eyes. We do not have as much reverence as we ought to have. We are not by nature or by training a reverent people. There are those who say we become less reverent as the years go on. The older people are constantly lamenting that they miss a certain beautiful respectfulness, a lovely reverence which were more common many years ago. There are wide areas of American society from which the spirit of reverence has been banished. Men and women in many a circle are clever, interesting, brilliant, but they lack one of the three dimensions of life: They have no reach upward. Their conversation sparkles, but it is frivolous and often flippant. Their talk is witty, but the wit is often at the expense of high and sacred things. He has come far down in the scale of being who, in order to display his powers, finds it necessary to ridicule those things which have been prized by all good men.

Possibly we are becoming less reverent because we are ashamed of being afraid of anybody or anything. Fear is one of the elements in reverence, and there is a popular impression that all fear is degrading. Fear is of two kinds—there is a godly fear and a fear which is ungodly. The latter has terror in it, and throws a shadow and brings a chill. But there is a fear which all unspoiled spirits feel in the presence of the high and holy. If mortal man, stained and marred by sin, is not awed by the thought of a Holy God, it is because he has lost the power of feeling. If there is a fear which degrades and paralyzes, there is also a fear which cleanses and exalts. The fear of the Lord is not only a virtue to be coveted by men, it is a grace lacking which angels and archangels would be incomplete. Reverence is the atmosphere of heaven. Let us come often then to the reverent Man of Nazareth who, by his awe-struck deference to his Heavenly Father, shames us out of our irreverence and makes it easier for the heart to kneel.

"Which one of you convicts Me of sin?"

JOHN 8:46 NASB

THE HOLINESS OF JESUS

Here for the first time in this course of sermons I use a word which belongs to another vocabulary. Courage, humility, patience, poise, brotherliness, indignation—these all belong to a common class, but we pass the boundaries into another region when we use the word "holiness." All the other words which I have used can be applied to many of the great men of the earth; the word "holiness" can be applied to one only: Jesus.

Heartfelt Questions

What do we mean by holiness? We mean "wholeness, full-orbed perfection." A holy man is a man without a fleck or flaw, a character without a blemish or a stain. Let us think about the sinlessness of Jesus. A thoughtful man might ask the question: "How do you know that he was sinless? You have only an account of his words and deeds, and while these may be above all criticism, how do you know what took place in the chambers of the heart? How do you know that every feeling was free from sin, that not a single thought was stained, that every motive, even the deepest, was according to the will of God? Do you not pass into the region of conjecture when you say that here was an absolutely sinless man?"

And the further fact might also be urged that we have the story of only a fraction of his life. He died at the age of thirty-three, and of this period thirty years are practically a total blank. Even if you grant that his public life was perfect, how can you speak with authority concerning the life which he lived before he appeared at the Jordan to be baptized by John? How do you know what his life was as a boy, as a youth, as a young man? Of all this period, scarcely a syllable is told us, and yet how many sins may have been committed in those seething, tempestuous years?"

> Never has there been but one pure soul, never but one life unspotted, never but one mind without a stain, never but one heart perfect. It is this sinlessness which gives Jesus his power.

And one might go on to say: "How can you be sure that all that he did and said recorded in the New Testament was absolutely right in the sight of God? When he denounced the Pharisees and hurled his cutting epithets at them, can you be sure there was no excess of passion? When he drove the traders from the Temple, can you be certain that he did not overstep the boundaries of righteous indignation? When he cursed the fig tree, was there no impatience in his words? When he drove the Syro-Phoenician woman away with the remark that it was not fitting to take the children's bread and cast it unto dogs, was he not guilty of the very sin which disfigured and disgraced so many of his country-men?"

And then again, "How can you be sure that he fulfilled every duty? Even granting that we cannot charge him with any sins of commission, how do you know there were no sins of omission? Duty is infinite. There are duties toward God and toward one's fellow-men and toward one's own soul, and who in this world is competent to say that Jesus fulfilled every duty to himself and to men and to God up to the level of perfection?" These are natural questions, and questions which deserve an answer. They will occur to thoughtful minds whenever they approach the question of Jesus' holiness.

Weighing the Evidence

In answer to these questions, it may be said, in the first place, that so far as we can discover, there is nothing in Jesus' consciousness which indicates that he was guilty of any sin. There is no trace anywhere of regret, no indication anywhere of remorse. From first to last he is serene, jubilant, confident and free, so far as we can see, from that shadow which the consciousness of sin always casts. Now everybody agrees that Jesus was a good man, exceedingly good, extraordinarily good. Everybody admits that he was the best man that ever lived. But if we once admit this, we are bound to go a great deal farther, for just in proportion as a man is really good does he become sensitive to sin; just in proportion as his spiritual sense is keen does his consciousness of sin become disturbing and appalling.

If you want the saddest confessions of shortcomings, do not go to the worst men, but to the best. The higher a man rises in spiritual attainment, the more is he cast down by the knowledge of his sins. Run through the Scriptures, and you will find that all the saints have their faces in the dust. Isaiah has a vision of God and his first cry is, "Woe is me! for I am undone" [Isaiah 6:5 KJV]. Job has a vision of God, and he casts himself upon the ground, saying, "I abhor myself and repent in dust and ashes" [Job 42:6 KJV]. John the beloved disciple says, "If we say we have no sin, we deceive ourselves, and the truth is not in us" [1 John 1:8 KJV]. Paul, the greatest of all the apostles, cries out in an agony of remorse, "I am the chief of sinners." Peter says, "Depart from me, for I am a sinful man, O Lord" [Luke 5:8 KJV]. There is no exception in the whole list from Abraham down to the latest of the apostles. Every heart cries out in the language of the Psalmist: "Have mercy upon me, O God...blot out my transgressions," and "wash me thoroughly from mine iniquity, and cleanse me from my sin, for...my sin is ever before me" [Psalm 51:1-3 KJV].

If, therefore, Jesus is, indeed, the best man that ever lived and still a sinner, he must have been conscious of his sin; and if he had been an honest man, conscious of his sin, he would not have concealed the fact from those that were nearest to him. He would have given signs of repentance and shown traces of regret. There would have been many an evidence of contrition and shame. But so far as any of the apostles knew, there never escaped his lips a cry for pardon. On the other hand he was always giving utterance to words like these: "He that hath seen me hath seen the Father" [John 14:9 KJV]; "I do always those things that please him" [John 8:29 KJV]; and "Which one of you convicts Me of sin?" [John 8:46 NASB]. And even when in sight of the cross, with death only a few hours away, he looks into God's face saying, "I have brought you glory on earth by completing the work you gave me to do" [John 17:4 NIV]. Other men looked into the unstained splendor, the white radiance of the world eternal, and fell back abashed and condemned; Jesus looks into that same unspotted glory and says, "I have finished the work which you gave me to do." This is remarkable, altogether unique.

Here is a man who told others to say when they prayed, "Forgive us our debts as we forgive our debtors" [Matthew 6:12 KJV], but he never prayed that prayer himself. Other men, even the strongest, have asked others to pray for them—he never asked prayers of any man. If then we are willing to listen to the consciousness of Jesus, we are bound to confess that here was a man without sin. If he was not without sin, then he was not a good man at all, for he carefully concealed from his companions the stained parts of his life and led them to think that he was better than he was, in which case he was a hypocrite and our hero has vanished.

But this is not all. Not only did he hold himself immeasurably above the heads of all other men, but he forgave sins—he spoke as one having authority. No other man had ever exercised such a pre-rogative. Even the worst sinners, when penitent at his feet, received from him authoritative assurance of forgiveness. Moreover, he was a man without a human ideal. All good men have looked up to some man better than themselves; Jesus looked up to no man. He placed himself above Moses. He said, "A greater than Solomon is here" [Luke 11:31 KJV]. He said to men, "Follow me, for I am the ideal." And at the same time he said, "Be ye therefore perfect, even as your Father which is in heaven is perfect" [Matthew 5:48 KJV]. How will you put these two exhortations together? "Follow me! Be ye perfect!" He was re-lentless at this point: He would not allow anyone to get between him and the soul. If he were indeed perfect, all this was right; but if he were a sinner concealing his sin or unconscious of his sin, then all such exhortations as, "Follow me," are demoralizing, and his preten-sions are blasphemous. If he was good at all, he was sinless.

Attention ought to be called to the impression which he made upon others. The men who were nearest to him got the idea that he was without sin. When he came to John the Baptist asking to be baptized, John drew back from him, saying: "I cannot baptize you. You ought to baptize me." And why? Because John was baptizing men for their sins. He could not baptize Jesus, because Jesus had no sins. And when Jesus makes his reply, he does not say, "I am a sinner, therefore I must be baptized," he says, "Suffer it now, for it is becom-ing that we should fulfill all righteousness." There was a reason why the baptism should be performed—there was another element in baptism besides confession of sin.

John was the beloved disciple, coming the nearest to the Master's heart. In the third chapter of his first letter he says this, "But you know that he appeared so that he might take away our sins. And in him is no sin," [1 John 3:5 NIV]. That was the impression which the Lord made upon him. Peter was one of his most loyal friends. He was with him day and night through three years. In the second chapter of his first letter he says, "[He] did no sin, neither was guile found in his mouth" [1 Peter 2:22 KJV]. Now these men were with Jesus. They ate with him, drank with him, slept with him. They saw him in all conditions and in all moods, and under varying circumstances. They saw him hungry, angry, stern, surprised, disappointed, amazed, yet they believed that in him there was no sin.

The writer to the Hebrews reminds his readers in chapter four that while Jesus was tempted in all points as we are, yet he was without sin. That was the impression, then, which was made upon the church. After the resurrection, they worshipped him as God. It is inconceivable that in so short a time a great body of intelligent men and women should have been worshipping him as God and singing hymns of praise to him if he had not made upon them the impression that he was holy.

Unquestionably Set Apart

Here, then, we have reached the crowning characteristic of Jesus. It is this which differentiates him from all other men who have ever lived. Every other man has known the pang of remorse; every other man has cried for pardon. Simon Peter was hounded by memories; he was a good man, a great man, a tireless worker in the church, but condemning memories pursued him down through the years. And when at last the time came to die he said, "Crucify me with my head downward." He said this because he remembered his sin. Paul was a good man and a great man, but he was hounded by condemning memories. He filled the days and nights with work for God, but he could never forget that he had been a persecutor of the church, and so he entered heaven feeling that he was the chief of sinners. Never has there been but one pure soul, never but one life unspotted, never but one mind without a stain, never but one heart perfect. It is this sinlessness which gives Jesus his power.

We cannot understand the New Testament unless we acknowledge that he was holy. His life was one of suffering and persecution, ending in a horrible death, but the New Testament is a joyous book. There is no gloom in it because there was no gloom in him. His soul was radiant. Nothing creates gloom in this world but sin. All the things which we count terrible are insignificant and have no power to cast a shadow. There is only one thing which makes the spirit droop, and that is sin. His sinlessness explains his joyfulness. He said, "No man knows the Father but the son." Why? Because "blessed are the pure in heart: for they shall see God" [Matthew 5:8 KJV]. Because his heart was stainless, his vision of the Eternal was unclouded. He knew God as no other man has ever known him. And it was this sinlessness which was the secret of his attraction. He drew men to him; they hung upon his words; they were fascinated by him, even when they hated; they were drawn to him, even when they feared him. Simon Peter expresses the conflicting emotions of the heart in, "Depart from me; for I am a sinful man, O Lord" [Luke 5:8 KJV]. When Jesus asks him whether he is going away, he says, "To whom shall we go? You have words of eternal life" [John 6:68 NASB].

The reason we are drawn to him is not because of his courage, his sympathy, his patience, or his brotherliness; it is because we feel instinctively that he is far above us, a man without a sin. It is this which gives the Christian church its power. The Christian church has but one perfect possession: Jesus. The creed of the church is not perfect; its phrases were formed by the blundering mind of man. The church itself is imperfect, stained through and through with sin; but Jesus of Nazareth, the head of the church, is stainless. And because he is without sin, the church will come off triumphant.

"His name shall be called Wonderful."
ISAIAH 9:6 KJV

THE GREATNESS OF JESUS

What is greatness? Who is a great man? What is the distinctive element in a man which gives him this proud distinction? The dictionaries will not help us. What characteristic is common to all men whom history deems great? In such a heterogeneous company is it possible to find any mark which makes them akin? It is possible, and the quality which is common to all is an extraordinary capacity for achievement. These men all did things, enduring things, so that the world was not the same after they had gotten done with it. They carved statues or painted pictures or led armies or ruled states or composed music or framed laws or wrote poems or made discoveries or inventions which enriched the lives and homes of men. They made a mark on the mind of the world. The product of their genius is an imperishable possession of [the human] race.

What Did He Achieve?

Was Jesus great? What did he achieve? What did he ever do? He never chiseled a statue or painted a picture or wrote a poem or composed a piece of music or constructed a philosophical system or published a book or led an army or controlled a senate or framed a law or made a discovery or contrived an invention or did any one of the things which have made the names of other men illustrious. He never wore a crown or held a scepter or threw round his shoulders a purple robe. He never held an office either in church or state. He did absolutely nothing in art, literature, science, philosophy, invention, statesmanship or war—the seven kingdoms in which the world's great men have won their crowns. And yet everybody calls Jesus great. No informed man in any part of the world would today deny him that exalting adjective. Not only is he counted great, but in a large part of the world he is counted greatest—so great that no one else can be compared with him. Charles Lamb gave expression to the feeling of us all when he said, "If Shakespeare were to come into this room, we should all rise up to meet him; but if Christ was to come into it, we should all fall upon our knees." His greatness is greater than that of all others, and it is also different.

> Other great men are great artists or poets or generals or statesmen, whereas Jesus is a great man. His greatness lies in the realm of personality, in the kingdom of character.

Other men are great artists or poets or generals or statesmen, whereas Jesus is a great man. His greatness lies in the realm of personality, in the kingdom of character. His achievement was not wrought with paint or with chisel or with sword or with pen, but by the heavenly magic of a victorious will. There is nothing of him but his manhood. He wore none of the spangled robes of earth. We do not say, "Behold the poet, the orator, the philosopher, the general, the statesman, the sovereign"; we say, "Behold the Man!"

It is one of the saddest of all surprises to discover on reading the biographies of the world's immortal workers how many of them have been narrow and superstitious, selfish and envious, sordid in their ambitions and groveling in their aims, achieving one significant or beautiful piece of work in the glory of which the shabbiness of their character has been swallowed up. Jesus was great in his soul. The dimensions of his mind and his heart were colossal. His spirit was regal, august, sublime.

Above the Crowd

Jesus had eyes which saw to the core of every problem and to the center of every situation. He never missed the essential point or was misled by a subordinate issue. He stripped off the accidental from the soul of the essential, and no matter how tangled or complicated a matter was, he seized the dominant principle and made all things plain. Compared with him, the Scribes and Pharisees were owls batting their eyes in the glare of noon. Insight is a trait of greatness. Only great men see deep into things. It was his insight which made him formidable to the men who tried to trip and trap him with their questioning. Again and again they tried it, but they never succeeded. He always outwitted their subtlety, and always discomfited them at their favorite game. Whenever they dashed at him with a question intended to roll him in the dust, he seized it, turned its point upon the man who asked it and went on his way triumphant. Never did they get the advantage of him in a discussion or an argument. He was quick, dexterous, adroit, and yet when we think of him, we do not think of his cleverness because cleverness is a scintillation of the intellect, and while intellectual brilliancy dazzles us in other men, we are not impressed by it in Jesus because his cleverness is only one of many talents and endowments which combine to add luster to his princely, transcendent personality.

His greatness comes out in his fellowship with his disciples. They were strong and able men, all of them, able later on to turn the world upside down; but they cut a sorry figure in the presence of the man they acknowledge to be their master. They are pitifully and incorrigibly stupid. They cannot understand some of the simplest things the

Master says. He is so high above them that they cannot climb to where he is. There is pathos in his oft-repeated question, "Do you not yet understand?" But it is in their temper and ambition that the disciples are at the worst. They were petty, envious, selfish men. They wrangled among themselves as to which one of them should hold the highest place, and even on the last evening of Jesus' life they squabbled as to the places they should occupy around the table. No wonder he calls them "little children," for that was all they were. They were childish in their temper and ambitions—just as most men are. They were as old in years as Jesus; but in thought and aim, in hope and ideal, they were, as compared with Jesus, only a company of babies.

He Changed Lives

How great Jesus is can be told by the length and width and depth of his achievement. Greatness is measured by the effect which it produces. Men cannot be judged by stature or physical characteristics. You cannot tell whether a man is great or not by looking at his body. Nor can you find a man's greatness always in his words. Greatness does not lie in words but in souls. Not even do a man's actions reveal completely what he is. In their conduct great men act much as do ordinary men. It is by the total effect of a man's life that we are to tell whether or not he is great.

If Jesus is to be judged by the effects which he produced and still produces, then his name is indeed Wonderful. Upon the men of his time he exerted a power so marvelous that it seemed uncanny, magical, and some people thought he must be in league with the mighty powers of the underworld. When he spoke, men overflowed with ideas and feelings—feelings of love or feelings of detestation. No man ever stood stolid in his presence. Men went wild over him, some in adoration and some in hatred. Wherever he went, he left men seething and bubbling. There were a few men—his apostles—who came close to him. Upon these he exerted an influence which extended to the roots of their being.

One of the men—Thomas—was unusually slow and cool. He was not made of flammable stuff. He was not easily carried away by emotion, for the tides of emotion in him were not strong. But this man, when Jesus one day suggested going to a certain place beset with danger, exclaimed, "Let us go and die with him." It is not easy to die at thirty. No normal man in his ordinary mood wants to die before the sun has reached the meridian. But this man Thomas had been so wrought upon by the personality of Jesus that he was ready to die with him. Here is the pinnacle of power: Jesus changed men. He changed their habits and opinions and ambitions; he changed their tempers and dispositions and natures. He changed their hearts. They were never the same after they gave themselves up to him. God and man, the world and duty, were different to them after they had looked steadily into his face. Wherever he went, he transformed human lives. He transfigured human faces by cleansing the fountains of the heart. This is greatness indeed.

And what he did in Palestine, he has been doing ever since. Wherever the story of his life is carried, the climate of thought and feeling changes. Every land across which his name has been heralded has been transformed in ideals and institutions. The forward-looking portion of the world numbers the years from the date of his birth.

He Is the Image of God!

His greatness is full-orbed. He was full of grace and truth. He had a charm about him which wooed and fascinated. Children liked him, and Publicans hung upon him. He had the heart of a child, the tenderness of a woman and the strength of a man. The three dimensions of his life were complete. He had eyes which looked along extended lines, running into eternity; he had sympathies wide enough to cover humanity to its outermost edge; he had a purpose which included all lands and ages; his kingdom is to be universal, and it shall have no end. He is, at every point, complete. His virtues are all full-statured; his graces are all in fullest bloom. You can no more add anything to him than you can add something to the sky. He pushed every good trait of human character to its utmost limit. His forgiveness was unbounded; his generosity was untiring; his patience was inexhaustible; his mercy was immeasurable; his courage was illimitable; his wisdom was unfathomable; his kindness was interminable; his faith removed mountains; his hope had no shadow in it; and his love was infinite. So it is impossible to go beyond him.

We can never outgrow him. He will be always ahead of us. We shall always hear him saying, "Follow me!" He is the ideal of the heart. He is the goal of humanity. It is this completeness of his character which accounts not only for his beauty but for his perennial and increasing power. He is the image of God!

Who Are We?

Discipleship Publications International (DPI) began publishing in 1993. We are a nonprofit Christian publisher committed to publishing and distributing materials that honor God, lift up Jesus Christ, and show how his message practically applies to all areas of life. We have a deep conviction that no one changes life like Jesus and that the implementation of his teaching will revolutionize any life, any marriage, any family and any singles' household.

Since our beginning we have published more than 60 titles; plus we have produced a number of important, spiritual audio products. Almost one million volumes have been printed and our works have been translated into more than a dozen languages—international is not just a part of our name. Our books are shipped monthly to every inhabited continent.

If you would like to receive a complete catalog of our works, you can call toll free in the US, 1-888-DPI-BOOK. You can order other books listed on the following pages by calling the same number 24 hours per day. From outside the US, call 781-937-3883, ext. 231 during Boston-area business hours.

We appreciate the hundreds of comments we have received from readers. We would love to hear from you. Here are other ways to get in touch:

Mail: DPI, One Merrill St., Woburn, MA 01801
E-mail: dpibooks@icoc.org

Other Books from
Discipleship Publications International

9 to 5 and Spiritually Alive
A book for Christian women in the workforce
by Sheila Jones

Victory of Surrender
An in-depth study of a powerful biblical concept
by Gordon Ferguson

Mind Change: The Overcomer's Handbook
*For anyone who needs to overcome
any difficulty or challenge in life*
by Thomas A. Jones

Discipling
*A comprehensive teaching about
God's plan to train and transform his people*
by Gordon Ferguson

The Killer Within
*A riveting comparison of several
African diseases to the sin in our hearts and lives*
by Mike Taliaferro

Audio Products from Discipleship Publications International

Dating in the Kingdom
Biblical and practical help
from first date to going steady
by Jim and Teresa Brown

Working 9 to 5
Encouragement and input for
Christian working women
by Madaline Evans, Debby Miller,
Sheila Jones and Kim Walters

Real God—Real Men
Lessons from Genesis for men
by Sam Laing

Real God—Real Women
Lessons from Genesis for women
by Kay McKean

Walking with God
Developing a dynamic walk with God
by Russ Ewell

Out of the Pit
Healing the scars of the past
and learning a new way of thinking
by Dr. Hardy Tillman

More Than Conquerors
Breaking the bonds of the past
and becoming all God meant for us to be
by Dr. Hardy Tillman

Draw Near to God
Growing closer to God as we grow
older in our faith
by Gordon Ferguson

For information about ordering
these and many other resources from DPI,
call
1-888-DPI-BOOK
or from outside the US
617-938-7396.

World Wide Web
http://www.dpibooks.com